MW01100977

Strategic Management Simplified

What Every Manager Needs to Know
About Strategy and How to Manage it

Dr. Sidney L. Barton

iUniverse, Inc.
New York   Bloomington

iUniverse books may be ordered through booksellers or by contacting:

iUniverse
1663 Liberty Drive
Bloomington, IN 47403
www.iuniverse.com
1-800-Authors (1-800-288-4677)

Because of the dynamic nature of the Internet, any Web addresses or links
contained in this book may have changed since publication and may no longer be
valid. The views expressed in this work are solely those of the author and do not
necessarily reflect the views of the publisher, and the publisher hereby disclaims
any responsibility for them.

ISBN: 978-1-4401-9419-1 (sc)
ISBN: 978-1-4401-9421-4 (ebook)
ISBN: 978-1-4401-9422-1 (dj)

Library of Congress Control Number: 2009913249

Printed in the United States of America

iUniverse rev. date: 01/06/2010

Dedicated to my loving wife, Judith, without whose understanding and encouragement I never could have pursued my dreams.

Contents

Introduction

Although I have only recently begun to organize my thoughts and experiences in a single manuscript, in reality this book has been under development for over forty years. It represents the culmination of my experiences in industry and academia. The portfolio of experiences includes developing strategy as a young manager, researching strategy as an academic, teaching countless undergraduate, graduate, and executive education courses, and finally consulting with numerous organizations to develop strategy. During this entire time, I have been seeking to understand the most effective way to develop and manage strategy.

My early work experience was in a small, private firm where operational planning took our top managers a few months' time at the end of every year. The result was a lengthy tome that sat on our shelves but was hardly ever consulted until the time came to prepare the next year's plan. The basic problem with this approach was that almost as soon as the plan document was done, the world changed. Different opportunities, unexpected problems, and the economy were just some of the sources of change that made the plan obsolete. The result was that we intuitively reacted to the changed environment without being effectively assisted by our "plan" or the process we used to develop it. This plan was basically a detailed "budget," but it did not provide me with the assistance I was seeking in my daily decision making.

Another fundamental problem with this approach was that after doing it for a few years, everyone merely updated the previous year's plan without taking the time to examine if these activities were the best things we could be doing. In effect, it became just another task that needed to be done but had little impact on our daily activities. It was never referred to when making resource allocation decisions on new issues or opportunities. The good aspect of the process was that it forced management to spend some time thinking about what we needed to achieve in revenues and cost containment to meet our sales and profit goals for the year. However, this exposure to budgetary planning left me with a desire to find something that would provide meaningful direction to the organization without taking so much management time to develop.

In addition to my "in-house" experience, my job allowed me to be exposed to some of the largest firms in the world. As a manager of technical sales, I was able to interact and observe the strategic approaches and results of these firms. My experiences suggested that for most of these firms there did not appear to be a well-developed and coordinated overall strategy guiding their technology decisions. In many cases the actions and decisions of the technical people did not seem to be related to the stated "strategy" of these organizations. This fact also piqued my curiosity with respect to how to manage better the strategic direction of firms.

After thirteen years in this environment, I left my practitioner job and went back to school to get a PhD in strategic management. This experience opened my eyes to exactly what strategy is and, most importantly, how personal decision making is so central to the concept. It provided me with a totally different perspective on the concept of strategy for organizations.

The combination of the practitioner and academic researcher perspectives motivated me to develop an approach to strategy that would address the problems I had observed as a practitioner. First, any process would need to provide meaningful, real-time direction for individual resource allocation decision making throughout the organization. Second, it would need to be developed reasonably quickly to allow small organizations to utilize the concept effectively and large organizations to adapt quickly. Third, it would need to be continuously adaptable to the many environmental and organizational changes that constantly occur. And last, it would need to be understandable and actionable by employees at all levels of the organization.

I utilized the research and academic knowledge and practical experiences I had been exposed to and developed an approach to strategic management that I believed would address these criteria. I refined my understanding of the process and my approach as I applied the techniques successfully to both for-profit and not-for-profit organizations.

The result is the material presented in this book. Chapter 1 outlines how I define the strategy concept as a basis for the rest of the book. Chapter 2 discusses several characteristics and managerial policies of organizations that have been shown to be essential context for successful strategic management in both the formulation and implementation stages of strategy. Chapter 3 develops a set of desired outcomes that should result from any successful strategic management system. Chapter 4 presents a strategic decision making framework and its various elements that I have found to be useful in making such decisions. Chapter 5 then introduces a very simple management process for implementing the framework and addressing the criteria set out in chapter 3. Finally, chapter 6 provides examples of the experiences of real organizations where I have personally facilitated utilizing this approach. (I must add here that I am indebted to the three organizations included for allowing me to share their strategies with outsiders.)

A simple caveat is that virtually every organization that attempts to manage strategically wonders if they are optimally using their time and resources, regardless of what process or approach they are using. Along with the many books on the topic, virtually every consultant of strategic planning (and there are thousands) recommends a different process or set of tools. Most practitioners have tried various processes and methods (as well as consultants) until they settle on a method that at least seems most effective. The fact is that there are as many different processes and tools for developing and implementing strategic planning as there are organizations. In other words, managers modify basic strategy processes and tools to best fit their specific organization, culture, external environment, personal preferences, managerial philosophies, and styles. [1]

My experience over the years suggests that the model I propose is no different. In fact, virtually every organization I have worked with has started with my model and taken what worked for them to develop their own unique, individualized approach. The key to these modified approaches was a fundamental belief in the underlying philosophy that is the foundation of this model. What I sincerely hope will result is that the ideas and concepts introduced in this book will at least force you to think about how you are currently doing strategic planning. If the ideas presented herein resonate with you, perhaps you can use some of the model. If you have never done any strategic planning, and the ideas presented make sense to you, I suggest that you start with this model and build

---

1   Knott, P. (2008). "Strategy tools: Who really uses them?" *Journal of Business Strategy* 29(5): 26–31.

on it as you go. If you don't subscribe to the basic management philosophy implied in the book, I strongly suggest that you stay with what you currently are doing. On the other hand, if these points don't fit your idea of good management practices I doubt you will need my advice to reject the approach outright.

Lastly, just a word about why I use the term strategic management instead of strategic planning. The clear implication is that strategy is ever changing in response to changes in the organization and the external environment. As such, it is very much a dynamic phenomenon. The term "plan" implies a static (or point in time) exercise, while the term "management" suggests interaction and responsiveness to dynamic context. All kinds of plans can be developed to lead action, but they should be based on a strategy for the organization. The challenge is to actually manage the organization's strategy over time and to think strategically as you are doing it. Therefore, for the remainder of the book, strategic planning (strategy formulation) is subsumed as part of an overarching strategic management concept that includes both formulation and implementation. As Andrews put it, *"Strategic management* is … the administration of operations dominated by purpose and consideration of future opportunity, with explicit attention given to the need to clarify or change strategy as results suggest and to enter the future on a predetermined course. *Strategic planning*, if used with strategic management, usually refers to the staff apparatus of long-range planning."[2]

This book attempts to provide guidance for organizations that desire to maximize their performance by suggesting management practice and a specific model of strategy formulation and implementation that is informed by academic research and my own extensive experience. The concepts in

---

2   Andrews, K. R. (1980). *The Concept of Corporate Strategy.* Homewood, IL: Richard D. Irwin, p. viii.

the book apply equally well to large and small organizations as well as to for-profit and not-for-profit groups. I hope that no matter what kind of organization you belong to you will find the information to be helpful in your quest to manage the organization strategically.

Chapter 1: Strategy Basics

The purpose of this chapter is to establish for the reader just how I view the concept of strategy. It will become apparent as you read through the manuscript that these basic elements provide a system of beliefs that are the foundation of the proposed approach to strategy found in the remainder of the book.

Definition

What exactly is "strategy"? There are lots of definitions, but my favorite was penned by Kenneth Andrews in 1980. He declared that "corporate strategy is the pattern of decisions in a company that determines and reveals its objectives, purposes, or goals (and) produces the principal policies and plans for achieving those goals ..." [1]

The reason I like this definition so much is that it best represents what really happens as opposed to what theoretically *should* happen in organizations. In effect, it states that what are most important are one's actions (decisions) and not what one says their goals and strategy are. While strategy is normally thought of as being developed prospectively, the reality is that as our situation changes and moves, we intuitively react to

---

1   Andrews, K. R. (1980). *The Concept of Corporate Strategy.* Homewood, IL: Richard D. Irwin, p. 18.

attempt to best achieve our desires. Often (almost always) these reactions are not necessarily consistent with our initial point of departure. The result is that when articulating strategy, we retrospectively assess what we did in order to adequately and rationally explain it. In essence this definition recognizes the dynamic, ever-changing nature of strategy. In a parallel way, a person's career is very similar. Often we end up at the end of our working lives having experienced a very different career than we might have envisioned when starting. This is caused by the fact that individuals change, as does the environment they find themselves in. But in any event, at the end of our working lives, everyone has had a "career," whether planned or not. (This reality is often cited by skeptics of formal strategic planning as a good reason not to do it at all. The argument is that if a plan is going to change soon after it is developed, then why bother doing it in the first place. Chapter 2 addresses the reasons and value of such planning.)

As an example of this, the engineering company where I started my career began simply as a structural testing firm. The initial "strategy" was to utilize sophisticated testing equipment to identify complex mechanical problems and suggest solutions. Over time, computer capabilities allowed us to model mechanical structures and predict performance before prototypes were built to avoid field problems. Initially, the software we developed was primarily used to evaluate the structural modifications suggested by our testing. Instinctively, resources were committed to take advantage of these new capabilities and address an even bigger client need, design analysis. We then began offering these software capabilities to our clients for their own use. Very quickly, we became a computer software firm as well as a troubleshooting testing firm.

Further improvements in computer power and software capabilities eventually allowed the firm to commit resources to allow more efficient modeling of structures and more efficient analysis by ourselves and our clients. Eventually, the firm also developed project management software that allowed clients to collaborate on mechanical system design among multiple locations. None of these steps was envisioned a priori by management, but the current firm is a multi-billion-dollar enterprise that looks nothing like what was initially envisioned.

In retrospect, the "strategy" can easily be described. We started by understanding mechanical system behavior via testing. Through this testing capability we were able to develop and verify computer simulation software that allowed us to more efficiently develop fixes for the problems we identified. Once software was effective at simulating existing systems, the next logical step was to use it to evaluate designs of systems before they were built. To make the analysis software easier to use and faster, modeling software was developed. Finally, with the capability to simulate system performance at the drawing-board stage, software to allow multiple designers to collaborate in product development provided even more convenience and usability.

The point of this example is that our technology and client needs changed significantly through time. Decisions were made along the way that took advantage of these changes, and thus the "strategy" changed. This example will be referred to often in the rest of the book, as it will allow me to make important points along the way.

Utilizing this definition and its implications, coupled with my own experiences in developing strategy over the years, the remainder of this chapter lists what I call "words of wisdom" related to strategic management. These are a few things about strategic management that need to be understood to provide a solid foundation for the process later developed. They represent a set of beliefs and a philosophy that permeate the remainder of the book.

Actions Equal Strategy

I recall a meeting many years ago where I was instructing a large group of managers on strategy concepts. After discussing the above definition of strategy, I asked the managers to state the single most important goal of the firm. Without hesitation, the assembled group shouted out "quality," as if orchestrated by some unseen conductor. The unanimity of the response was impressive (as I will discuss later); however, I followed up the question with a scenario designed to validate the group's initial response.

The company in this example manufactured very large mechanical systems that individually were worth millions of dollars. The scenario posited was as follows. It is near midnight on December 31 of a particular year. The firm's fiscal year is the calendar year, so this is the last day of the year. On the plant floor sits a huge system ready to ship to a valued client. If the system can be shipped out before midnight, the firm will make their yearly sales and profit goals. If it cannot be shipped and invoiced, the firm will fall short of these goals. Unfortunately, a significant problem has been identified with the machine. It is clearly not up to the quality standards of the firm and cannot be fixed by midnight. What will happen? Will the firm ship the system or wait until it meets the firm's quality standards, thus validating the stated preeminent goal?

For the longest time, there was total silence from the group. Finally, one brave soul in the rear of the room yelled, "We would ship it, but we would fix it in the field!" Laughter ensued, but the point was made. Quality was obviously important to the firm, but not as important as sales and profit.

The point of this example is not to say that sales and profit are not reasonable or appropriate goals. But what it does suggest is that what is most revealing about strategy are the choices we make when confronted with alternative courses of action. These choices, taken together, clearly reveal what we want and how we want to obtain it.

In another example, while assisting a software firm in deciding which operating system they should use for future development, the following took place: I inquired of the software manager what the best operating system would be for their product line. He responded that he felt that operating system "X" represented the future. I then asked him how many software engineers he had and how many were assigned to system "X" and how many to the current system, "Y." After some review of assignments, the answer was that of the 125 engineers assigned to software development, 25 were assigned to "X" and 100 were assigned to "Y." Obviously, while he may have felt intellectually that he was moving his product to the new system, he *actually* was favoring continued development on the current system. This realization caused the manager to totally reassess his "strategy" but this time based on what he was doing versus what he *thought* he was doing.

Every Organization Has a Strategy

Another important aspect of this definition is that even if a specific strategy is never formally written or articulated by the top management, the firm *has* a strategy. Obviously, decisions get made every day as to what to do and how to do it; thus the pattern of these decisions clearly "reveals the goals and means to achieve them." The question then becomes, "Does a formalized strategic management process really make a difference in firm results?" Research overwhelmingly says that it does make a significant, positive difference. [2]

2 Andersen, T. J. (2000). "Strategic planning, autonomous actions and corporate performance," *Long Range Planning* 33(2): 184–200.

While this result should encourage you to actively pursue formalized strategic management, the research does not discriminate among various types or degrees of sophistication of the processes employed. Obviously, the more effective and efficient the process, the better the results one should expect. Unfortunately, formal strategic management by itself does not guarantee success but merely that you are better off with it than without it.

When I teach strategic management to students or executives, I often use the analogy of a boat. Some firms are like large ocean-going vessels that have difficulty turning around in a short time or distance. Other, smaller firms may be much more mobile than the big boats but can be capsized if they get in the big boat's wake. In any event, if your boat has lots of holes, is old, or sails in rough waters, the best strategic management may do is to keep you afloat a bit longer than if you did no planning. The problem for most of us is that once we are on a singular type of boat for a while, it is very difficult to change to another type of boat. Thus we had better do the best we can in the boat we find ourselves.

Therefore, a formalized process of strategic management does indeed improve a firm's chance of success, but it cannot *guarantee* it.

Strategy Is Based on Critical Assumptions of the Strategist

Because strategy plays out in the form of resource allocation decisions, the clear implication is that individuals make these decisions. Further, since individuals are limited by "bounded rationality" (i.e., they cannot realistically have all the facts they need to make a decision), they must often make these decisions with less than complete information.

A very personal example of this occurred for me while I was vice president of sales and marketing for the previously mentioned engineering consulting and software firm. At one point in the firm's history, the chairman and founder of the firm believed strongly that our firm should set up service centers across the country so that our customers could better utilize our software and consulting services. He made the decision based on an *assumption* of client need. No formal market research information was sought out to validate the basic premise of the decision. The only information came from the intuition of the CEO based on his own experiences and observations. Unfortunately, the assumption proved false. The company came close to bankruptcy, and the CEO eventually was forced out of the company he had created.

One possible lesson learned from this experience is that appropriate market research would have kept this error from occurring. However, market research is not necessarily the "magic bullet" that would solve this problem. It does not guarantee that the basic underlying assumption relevant for a strategic decision will be discovered or even maintained over time.

An example of just such a situation is the decision of Levi Strauss to enter the men's suit portion of the clothing market. This story was told as part of a management teaching video that I used several years ago in one of my strategy classes. The video featured actual Levi Strauss management personnel in action.

The rationale to explore this potential market was that Levi Strauss had a very recognizable and positive brand image with young males based on their casual jeans. The idea was to utilize that brand equity to move into the formal-attire portion of the market. The brand manager for the product theorized that Levi could utilize their existing distribution system (generally retail department stores) to effectively go after this market.

As a member of a large and sophisticated firm, the brand manager had some prototypes of the suits developed and proceeded to have professionally run focus groups evaluate the idea. A video record of what transpired was made, not only of the focus groups but also of the brand manager's reaction to the focus groups as he stood behind a one-way mirror. The result was highly revealing of the power and importance of the mind of the strategist.

The focus group participants, as one would suppose, were selected based on the demographics representative of the target market identified by the brand manager. They were presented with the idea of Levi Strauss selling men's suits through department stores. The fundamental question posed to these young men was "Would you buy these products in a department store?" The reaction was universally negative. Various individuals stated that they did not purchase suits in department stores but rather at boutiques and specialty stores. They also could not relate to buying a formal suit from a company known for making jeans.

Based on this reaction, a logical presumption would be that the brand manager would conclude that his assumptions were not valid and shut down the project. However, that was not the reaction at all. The video records that the brand manager, talking to his assistant during these focus groups, stated that these people were not telling the truth. He rationalized they were young men trying to impress the other young men in the groups and were embarrassed to admit that they actually would buy a Levi suit in a department store.

As amazing as this seems, despite this universal bad feedback, Levi went ahead with the project. As you might guess, it was an abject failure.

These two very different examples illustrate two important points about strategy. First, decisions get made based on assumptions of causal relationships. In other words, resources are committed based on what we think the result of those decisions will be. In the case of my CEO, he clearly believed that clients of our firm would want and need to access our products and services at a service center near their firm's location. The Levi's product manager clearly believed that young men would buy Levi suits in department stores because of the convenience and price. Unfortunately for both men and their firms, these assumptions were proven false in the harsh reality of the marketplace.

Second, because humans make decisions, these decisions are subject to human psychology and limitations. The two examples illustrate this point, but there are countless other examples that are well chronicled throughout history. Recall Hitler's fatal mistake to not commit enough Panzer divisions to counter the Allied invasion on D-day. This decision has been validated as being based on his belief (assumption) that this was merely an Allied diversion and not the real Allied invasion force. Couple this with his maniacal egotism, and we see how critical and key human cognitive attributes are to strategic decision making.

Thus, strategy is based on critical assumptions of individuals and the limitations of human beings to understand and interpret them.

Summary

The points outlined in this chapter are intended to establish the strategy concept and some important attributes from my own perspective. The next chapter describes management policies, practices, and style that have been shown to be important for successful strategy formulation and implementation.

Chapter 2: Supportive Policies and Managerial Environment

Academic research, combined with my own experience, has revealed a few organizational characteristics and managerial approaches that have been shown to be important to maximizing the success of any strategy or strategic management system. The following sections explain these points and provide real-life examples of their implementation.

No "Sacred Cows"

Because objective reality is a critical aspect of effective strategy, no issue or topic can be off-limits to analysis or discussion. This is akin to the classic "emperor without clothes" story we are all familiar with. Unfortunately, many times in businesses or organizations the leader has one or more sensitive topics that are just "off-limits" to discussion. In family businesses, the topic may be the lack of capability of a family member in the firm. Or it could be that a product or service is not performing well but top management insists that the poor results are caused by the lack of effort or skill of the sales force and not the lack of customer interest in the fundamental product or service.

Recall the story of my boss from chapter 1, the CEO of the engineering firm who committed significant resources of the firm to deploy physical service centers across the country based on an incorrect assumption. As the chief sales and marketing executive for the firm, I had the assignment of promoting this concept through our client base and the sales force. After a time, the feedback from our clients and sales force was unanimous. The clients were not ready for this service and could not see value in it. Consequently, we were not generating any sales. When I reported this to the chairman, his reaction was that we were not properly convincing the client of the inherent value of the service. In other words, we were not working smart or hard enough.

He was convinced that he was correct and would not entertain any further discussion of the project. Unfortunately, these centers required significant investment in hardware and personnel. He went forward with the project, and despite our (and his) best efforts, no appreciable sales developed. As mentioned before, the ultimate result was that the firm came close to bankruptcy and the chairman was forced out of the firm he had started and grown successfully.

Research suggests this *sacred cow* phenomenon can lead to the stifling of innovation and is one important reason that firms fail.[1] Ironically, the more successful an organization becomes, the more susceptible it is to this phenomenon. An old Chinese proverb says that if you want to destroy a man, give him forty years of good luck. He then begins to think he knows all the answers, doesn't listen to objective reality, and commits fatal mistakes as a result. As for me, I don't think the phenomenon requires forty years.

---

1   Amatucci, F. M., & Grant, J. H. (1993). "Eight strategic decisions that weakened Gulf Oil," *Long Range Planning* 26(1): 98–110. Miller, D. (1993). "The architecture of simplicity," *Academy of Management Review* 18(1): 116–138.

I ran across another example of this situation during a consulting engagement with a small family firm. The firm was attempting to develop a marketing strategy as part of an overall corporate strategy. The president was adamant that the key to their sales growth was to generate as many cold calls as possible on prospective clients. The sales manager was equally adamant that the key was to pursue and develop further business with current clients and utilize referrals from these clients to get new business.

Apparently, this disagreement had been going on for years. I know, you would assume that the president would have replaced the sales manager long ago, but rationality is not always operative in business, especially family business. This was a topic that could not be discussed rationally, and therefore it was never resolved.

As a consultant, I had insisted that I could not participate in their process if any issue was off-limits. Having agreed to this demand a priori, the president was duty bound to address the issue. I requested that the sales manager retrieve the client list. We then examined the 20 percent of their clients that made up the top 80 percent of the firm's business. For each client, from the largest to smallest based on sales, the president and sales manager recalled how they obtained the business. In every case, it was a referral from another good client. Red-faced, the president conceded that indeed previous cold-call efforts that he had pushed and demanded had been less than successful.

The value of this realization was that a more useful marketing strategy could be developed. Instead of developing mass marketing pieces and expensive advertising programs to attract new business, the plan focused on account management activities and targeted marketing pieces for referral clients. A sacred cow was thus eliminated from the firm, and more success followed.

While this requirement may seem easily obtained, my experience suggests otherwise. Many CEOs do not want to be challenged in areas where they may feel unsure of or unable to articulate a solid rationale. They trust their intuition but often cannot easily explain the basis for their feelings. They often feel that they "know what is right when they see it" but cannot explain why.

As mentioned above, before taking an assignment as a strategic planning facilitator, I always insist on talking to the CEO of the organization to make sure they are willing to have any issue or topic honestly evaluated and openly discussed. I recall one such interview that was going extremely well until I raised this point. Immediately, the CEO changed the subject to our sons and daughters and what they were doing with their lives. At that point the business side of the discussion was over, and I knew we would not be working together.

The fact is that if the CEO does not share this philosophy with the facilitator, the facilitator can cause more harm than good. This is because participant expectations of full disclosure in the process will at some point be rendered impossible, thus causing more resentment and disappointment than may already be present. In fact, the reason I require agreement from the CEO on the *no sacred cows* policy provides another illustration of the problem.

Several years ago, a large manufacturing firm developed a management training program utilizing external experts from the area. Participants in the program were selected based on management's assessment of their potential for higher management positions in the firm. These folks were considered fast-trackers and the "cream of the crop" in this company.

I was asked to develop the strategic planning segment of the curriculum. I was contacted by the VP of administration for the company. We met several times to discuss their situation and what he wanted to accomplish. We finally agreed that I would present an outline of a strategic positioning statement for their firm based on their perception of past decisions made by the firm (i.e., deducing the strategy from the "stream of decisions" they had observed.) The assignment for the participants was to develop this strategy statement and then apply it to a current potential acquisition opportunity. They were to develop a recommendation based on this evaluation.

As a follow-up to this assignment, the VP agreed to present the actual firm's strategy statement and apply it to the same opportunity, thus revealing the actual strategic rationale of the firm and bringing the concepts home to the participants in a very meaningful way.

My session took place in the morning. When I presented the day's agenda to the class, they were visibly excited and motivated. They were going to have an opportunity to get a first-hand look at the firm's thinking and future direction. Things went very well.

After my session and during lunch, the VP joined me. He had some disturbing news. Apparently, as he was preparing for his afternoon session that morning, the CEO had stopped in to inquire about the program. The VP proudly told the CEO what was planned and how excited he was to interact with these top employees. At that point the CEO informed him that he was not to share any strategic information with these folks, nor was he to entertain any input from these people about the potential acquisition.

Fortunately for me, I was not invited to attend the afternoon session. After all, the plan was to share the firm's strategy, and as an outsider, there was no good reason for my presence. However, I had raised the expectations of these people that they would have an opportunity to have a meaningful discussion about the firm's strategy and its effect on a potential acquisition with an officer of the firm. They were clearly looking forward to the session. I wished the VP good luck facing these folks and admitted that I was glad I wasn't going to be there.

I do not know exactly what took place that afternoon, but I do know that I thought at that moment that this company was in big trouble. I can only surmise the surprise, disappointment, and frustration that this must have caused for those employees. Had I known ahead of time the attitude of the CEO, I would never have raised the expectations of these managers.

Today, that firm is a mere shadow of its once proud self and is facing reorganization. While I do not know all the factors involved in their ultimate decline, I can't help but think that this *sacred cow* attitude played some part.

Obviously, from that point forward, I always insist on the CEO's willingness to allow for all topics to be on the table for honest and open evaluation.

Accountability Required for Strategic Assignments

Many managers I have worked with over the years have had a problem with prioritizing assignments arising from a strategic management process. Admittedly, for most of these folks their regular operational assignments fully consumed their time, leaving not much for incremental "strategic" assignments. However, unless these assignments are taken seriously in terms of content and time to complete, the strategy-making process suffers considerably.

For clarification, a strategic assignment can be thought of as any one that is intended to better inform the decisions that are being contemplated by the organization but is not directly part of the operational activities of the assignee. Examples of such assignments I have observed include estimating market size for the organization's products, clarifying client needs, experimenting to challenge distribution or pricing assumptions, researching competitor products and strategies, and refining the organization's vision and mission statements.

In addition, before going further I need to add another important belief I hold with respect to strategic management. Most organizations do not have the slack resources to have non-line managers or consultants do effective strategic assignments like the examples listed above. For these organizations, which comprise the large majority of organizations in the world, line managers must carry out these strategic assignments. However, even for the ones that have extensive staff resources, the responsibility for decision making resides with the line management of the organization. As such, the responsibility for the organization's strategy rests with these managers. Therefore, my belief is that no matter what the size of the organization, line management must be intimately involved with strategy development and implementation if strategy is to be effectively managed.

To bring the reality of the problem home, consider a VP of sales who is charged with delivering a continual stream of revenues into the firm. This can be a very high-stress job. Now suppose they are asked to also develop some in-depth information on the nature of the firm's clients and how they may react to changes the firm is contemplating. Especially in small firms where significant numbers of subordinates are not available to be delegated aspects of the task, the VPs may have to do the entire task themselves.

The result is often that they beg forgiveness for not completing the project on time, or worse, they throw something together at the last minute to satisfy their assignment. Neither of these situations can be tolerated by the CEO if strategic management is to be taken seriously and thus be worthwhile.

When I think of the important dimensions of organization management, fundamentally there are two, operational and strategic. The first can be described as "doing things right." This is the operational dimension that every organization must focus on every day. Quality initiatives, weekly sales and production reviews, and continuous improvement programs represent a few examples of this dimension. The second dimension is "doing the right things." This is the strategic dimension. It is not something that is addressed nearly as often as the operational dimension, but for an organization to be maximally successful, it is perhaps more important than the operational dimension. Clearly if one is not pursuing those activities that they can best do to achieve their goals, then no matter how efficient they are in their day-to-day activities, they will not achieve what they want. The most efficient buggy whip manufacturer has long since gone out of business.

Thus, when a strategic assignment is given to managers, it must be treated just as importantly as any operational assignment by the CEO. This means that failure to complete or do poorly on such a project will result in real repercussions to the assignee, such as a negative impact on compensation or promotion. Real actions like these serve notice that strategic management is critical to success for the firm and that nothing short of best efforts will be tolerated.

Top Management Involvement

Responsibility for strategic management cannot be delegated to any person below the CEO of the organization. It is their job to lead the process. Otherwise, they abdicate the responsibility to determine the goals of the firm and how those goals will be achieved.

It becomes clear that only a CEO can assure that all topics are available for assessment (*no sacred cows*) and that executives are held to high standards when given a strategic assignment (accountability), including him or her self.

Jack Welsh, former CEO of General Electric Corporation, stated in an internal taped message to his employees that his sole job was to develop and articulate the strategy of the firm for all employees and make sure that they carried it out to the best of their abilities. Of course, not all ideas come from the CEO. Groups and individuals can be assigned to develop plans. However, the CEO must be actively involved in the process and is obviously responsible for the ultimate product.

In recognition of this role, the term "strategic management" is used to describe the role of the CEO in an organization. As we shall see later, the process of developing and implementing strategy is a continuous one that requires constant monitoring and action, just as operations management does.

Thus, for maximal strategic management effectiveness the CEO must be actively involved in the process and must view it as just as important as operations assignments.

A Culture That Encourages Challenges to Critical Assumptions Is Important for Strategic Management Success

A common characteristic of human beings is a dislike for having their belief system challenged. Because managers are people (or at least most are), they tend to have this same trait. This makes application of this point extremely difficult to achieve in any organization, as it goes against human nature. Another way to think of this is that we tend to interpret information through filters that are biased by our experiences and belief systems, and information that appears to contradict these beliefs is often discounted or rejected entirely as representing abnormalities or "outlier" events. In contrast, events that seem consistent with these beliefs are used to validate or "prove" the truth of the beliefs. Therefore, information deduced from data reflects the frame through which one looks. (Refer to the Levi Strauss example above.)

An example I often use in class to exemplify the point is as follows. Pretend you are walking down the street, and approaching you is a young woman dressed in a nun's habit. She is well groomed and politely smiles at you upon her approach. As you observe her passing you, you notice that she is coming upon a small bird on the sidewalk that appears to be hurt and unable to fly. Without warning or apparent provocation by the bird, the woman steps directly on the bird, crushing it with her shoe, and then continues down the street without stopping. How do you interpret what just happened?

Most students say that she probably was in deep thought and totally unaware of her surroundings. Otherwise, there is no way she would deliberately kill the bird.

Now suppose the scenario is the same, with the exception that the woman in the habit was replaced by a rough, unshaven, tattooed biker with chains around his neck. Further suppose that he gives you a menacing look as he passes. Again, the injured bird is in front of this person, lying helpless on the sidewalk. However, in this case, the biker stops to gently pick up the bird and place it in his pocket before he continues on.

Some students suggest he would take the bird to a secluded spot and torture it. Placing it in his pocket was merely a convenient act that would allow him more time to mess with the bird later.

In both cases, our predisposed prejudices influence our interpretation of the act. Our natural instinct is to discount the act as an outlier if it conflicts with our belief about certain types of people. This is as dangerous in a business as it is in our daily lives.

In a business setting, the engineering firm and Levi stories described above exemplify this problem. In spite of data presented to these managers that would seem to have contradicted their belief system, these folks chose to discount or ignore these data and forge ahead based on their flawed assumptions. The result was a failed strategy.

Unfortunately, most of us have the habit of highlighting validating data and ignoring or suppressing contradictory data. That is why most managers tend to "shoot the messenger" of bad news rather than embracing and learning from whatever the messenger brings.

However, if you examine this phenomenon, it becomes crystal clear why challenges to underlying assumptions are much more important than validating information. This is because validating information merely supports the continuation of what you are already doing. With or without it does not affect the continued implementation of the strategy. On the other hand, valid data that contradict your belief system should cause you to investigate further the validity of your assumption. It may not always cause you to change what you are doing, but at the very least it will provide you with valuable information that may assist you in being more successful in pursuit of your goals.

This means that the most effective strategic management systems must be accompanied by a culture that supports and encourages (rewards) challenges to the existent belief system. Admittedly, these challenges must be well documented and supported with data. It cannot simply be a different opinion. But when data like this are real, it can provide a significant opportunity to develop competitive advantage for the organization.

Thus the organization must encourage discovery of disconfirming data of critical assumptions to be truly effective.

A Culture That Encourages Creative Conflict

Consistent with the challenging of critical assumptions is the culture of responsible conflict. This means that for any major decision that needs to be made, management encourages multiple positions be heard. Academic research has consistently shown over the years that decision making is improved when there are conflicting ideas expressed.[2] Two approaches that are often used effectively are the devil's advocate approach and dialectical inquiry.[3]

In the devil's advocate approach, a CEO or manager puts forth a decision or plan. Another person or group is then charged with the role of critic of the plan or decision. This role is charged with looking for problems with the plan. Problems might include bad or incomplete information, inconsistency of information, or questionable assumptions. The devil's advocate then is charged with reporting the problems with the plan to the decision maker. The decision maker can then decide to go ahead or modify or totally redevelop the approach used. This approach is useful in surfacing critical assumptions but by its very nature tends to emphasize the negative aspects of any decision or plan.

2 Amason, A. C. (1996). "Distinguishing the effects of functional and dysfunctional conflict on strategic decision making: Resolving a paradox for top management teams," *Academy of Management Journal* 39(1): 123–148.
3 Mitroff, I. I., & Emshoff, J. R. (1979). "On strategic assumption-making: A dialectical approach to policy and planning," *Academy of Management Review* 4(1): 1–12.

Dialectical inquiry involves several steps. First, proposal and counter-proposal groups are formed around an important issue or decision. A review group containing the senior decision maker is then set up. The proposal group develops a plan or recommends a decision and compiles a set of key, critical assumptions that underlie the plan and provides them to the counterproposal group.

"The counterproposal groups should endeavor to develop a counter-plan, looking at each assumption and breaking it down to invent a plausible counter-assumption and using it to surface new data, re-interpret old data, and devise a counter-plan.

The review group is presented plans from the proposal and counter-proposal groups—either side outlining data and assumptions they consider important and probing weaknesses of the other side's plan. A facilitator maintains goodwill and prevents the competitiveness from becoming destructive. The review group is looking for further unmentioned assumptions that may be central to the theory behind the problem (or decision). Should arguments become repetitive the facilitator ends the debate and there is a break to socialize and reconnect on a personal level.

The total group now works together, led by the review group their aim is to generate a list of agreed-upon fundamental assumptions and the generation of a new plan. All the assumptions that featured highly in the debate are pooled. Unacceptable assumptions are weeded out, and where necessary, competing assumptions are either reworked so as to be acceptable to both sides or subjected to simple tests devised to make decisions between them. The group will require the skills and attitudes needed for coping with muddled problems—finding the exact problem, representing alternative maps, and employing humor, confidence, and enthusiasm to maintain the process."[4]

---

4   http://www.mycoted.com/Dialectical_Approaches

I have seen a modified version of this approach used effectively in a consulting firm I worked with. A decision needed to be made to determine what features would be included in the next version of technical software to be developed. The managers representing the software developers were adamant about the features they wanted, while the representatives of the technical sales group were equally adamant about a completely different set of features. In effect, they could not agree, and from a political power perspective, neither side was willing to give in or compromise.

The approach I used to defuse the acrimony and achieve a good result was to explain to both sides that each group had a perfectly legitimate reason to favor one set of features over another. The opinions were driven by unique experiences, training, and perceptions based on their own backgrounds, which in this case were very different between groups. I forced each group to list the assumptions that provided the foundation for their proposed features. The discussion then centered around the assumptions and where they arose from, as opposed to the specific feature proposed. Where agreement was reached with respect to an assumption, it became the basis for development of a feature. For the assumptions that could not garner consensus, teams of two (consisting of one from each group) were given the task of getting more data and information about the assumption and coming back with an agreed-upon conclusion.

The result of this activity was twofold. First, the team was able to ultimately agree on the best set of features for the product. More importantly, the culture of the organization was changed. By introducing the concept that no one had a corner on absolute truth and that each person was biased by their own unique set of experiences, a new environment of cooperation and collaboration was born in the firm.

Without question, better decisions are made (and thus better strategy created) when creative conflict is a part of the organization's culture.

Open-Book Management

In 1996, John Case formally introduced the concept with his book *Open-Book Management: The Coming Business Revolution*.[5] While the idea of sharing the financial performance of the private firm with employees had been around for a while, Case's book made the case that to be successful in today's business world it is necessary to have eager, willing employees who understand the implications of their actions on the organization's success. Case's theory was that letting the employees know the financial state of the business is a requirement to achieve that kind of behavior.

Obviously, this open-book idea has always been available to employees of single business public companies. But since 90+ percent or so of firms are a division of a larger public firm or are private, most organizations are not required to share financial information with anyone other than owners and directors.

The natural reaction of owners of private firms is to restrict release of financial information. They cite problems like undue leverage for union employees seeking higher wages and employees leaking financial information to competitors as reasons not to pursue the practice. Add these reasons to the natural desire to keep private finances private and it is easy to see why there is resistance to this practice. However, "The idea of sharing financial information can be especially effective for family-owned business ... The trust and teamwork it can build can be important at family firms where there may be concerns about issues of fairness and preferential treatment for family

---

5   Case, John (1996). *Open-Book Management: The Coming Business Revolution*. New York: Harper Collins Publishers.

members versus non-family members."[6] And, according to a recent study reported in this same *Los Angeles Times* article, revenue increased 2 percent faster in open-book firms versus their competitors.

There are numerous reference books that go into depth in explaining the details of an open-book system, but there are a few basic steps in the process. First, determine what information is essential for employees to have to make good decisions. (Note that most plans do not provide access to sensitive salary data, as that is not necessary to make most decisions assigned to employees.) Second, provide training so that employees can properly interpret the information they will receive. Third, provide the information in an easily accessible format. Fourth, show the employees how their job impacts the numbers and give them responsibility over the numbers within their control. Last, give the employees some stake in the outcomes, whether it be salary increases, bonuses, or stock options.

In my own experience, I am on the board of directors of a mid-sized, private family-owned firm that has employed open-book management for several years. The result for them is an exceptional level of trust and commitment by employees that has resulted in virtually no voluntary turnover. Perhaps more importantly, the company is the unquestioned leader in its industry and commands leading market share position in every one of its product lines. In good years, everyone shares in the success through generous bonuses. In the tough years, of which there have been a few lately, everyone understands the tough decisions management has had to make to keep the firm viable. The environment in the organization is truly one of a team striving together to make everyone's life better.

---

6 Zwahlen, Cyndia (2000). "Company ledger an open book," *Los Angeles Times*, December 20, 2000. Quote from Karen Berman, founder of the Business Literacy Institute in West Los Angeles.

But you may be asking how this system specifically impacts the strategic management of the firm. The biggest reason is that managers and employees begin to see how their welfare is tied to the organization's success. They begin to think like "owners." By seeing how their jobs can affect the bottom line, they can better understand the overall strategy of the firm. This allows them to effectively participate in not only the implementation of the strategy but also in the formulation of the strategy. The trust that is developed between owners and employees that results from the combination of an open culture that encourages different ideas and the openness of financial disclosure creates a truly creative and positive environment for strategic management.

Maximum Involvement of Key Managers

Before discussing this point, it is important to define what I mean by a "key manager." These people are managers throughout the organization that have critically important information and understanding about what really happens day to day. As such, they become "key" because they are the ones who actually experience the resource allocation decisions being made. Based on the definition of strategy from chapter 1, this means they have frontline knowledge of the real strategy of the firm, so they are invaluable in making sure top management is not fooling itself about what is going on.

Often these folks are not included in the top management deliberations of strategy formulation. However, research suggests that actively seeking the knowledge that these folks possess has a very significant positive effect on performance.[7]

---

7 Floyd, S. W., & Wooldridge, B. (1994). "Dinosaurs or dynamos? Recognizing middle management's strategic role," *Academy of Management Executive* 8(4): 47–57. Floyd, S. W., & Wooldridge, B. (1997). "Middle management's strategic influence and organizational performance," *Journal of Management Studies* 34(3): 465–487.

In order to effectively include these individuals there must exist a culture of trust, and as discussed above, validatable disconfirming information must be rewarded. There also must be a perception of fairness and procedural justice present in the organization for these folks to enthusiastically and, more importantly, truthfully participate.[8]

The major advantage to including these managers in the strategy decision process is that if they feel that their input is honestly considered, there is a much higher commitment to implement the strategy.[9] This has the effect of making whatever strategy is formulated be successfully implemented throughout the organization. This is important, because whether the strategy is successful or not, if it is faithfully implemented the organization will know that the outcome was caused by the strategy and not by poor execution.

Another recommendation that is complementary to this one is to push strategic decisions down to the lowest level feasible in the organization. Particularly in the dynamic environments being experienced today, distributed decision authority to commit resources of the firm has significant positive effects on performance.[10] If the managers at these lower levels have been meaningfully involved in the strategy formulation process, they will be more committed to the implementation of the strategy

8   Kim, W. C., & Mauborgne, R. A. (1998). "Procedural justice, strategic decision making and the knowledge economy," *Strategic Management Journal* 19(4): 323–338.

9   Dooley, R. S., Fryxell, G. E., & Judge, W. Q. (2000). "Belaboring the not-so-obvious: Consensus, commitment and strategy implementation speed and success," *Journal of Management* 26(6): 1237–1257.

   Gerbing, D. W., Hamilton, J. G., & Freeman, E. B. (1994). "A large-scale second-order structural equation model of influence of management participation on organizational planning benefits," *Journal of Management* 20(4): 859–885.

10   Andersen, T. J. (2004). "Integrating decentralized strategy making and strategic planning processes in dynamic environments," *Journal of Management Studies* 41(8): 1271–1299.

because they participated in its development. [11] As will be seen in the following chapter, outstanding communication in the organization and a well-understood strategic decision making framework are important to the success of this approach.

Data-Driven Decision Making

Finally, one of the most important managerial policies to facilitate successful strategic management should be the insistence on collecting data to assess how the organization is doing. For many small firms, this is one of the most difficult habits to develop. As long as sales are coming in reasonably well, the tendency is to just keep doing what we have been doing, only a little faster. The problem with this attitude is that without data, learning cannot take place. And without learning, improvement cannot take place.

Without assumptions about causal relationships we do not have enough information to know without any doubt that certain actions result in certain other reactions. The only way we can test these assumptions is to gather data with respect to these relationships.

I refer to the example of my boss from the last chapter who wrongly assumed that clients needed computer service centers. In that case, a simple market survey, objectively analyzed, could have averted a major error that almost sank the firm. But any useful strategic management system will require measuring how the firm is doing in order to make good decisions. For example, what is the trend of repeat sales, sales to new clients, and sales of new products and services, to name a few pieces of useful data. What is the level of customer satisfaction with your products and services? If these data are important to making good decisions for the firm, then the data must be collected and

---

11   Ibid., p. 9.

analyzed. More importantly, once the data are analyzed, the conclusions must inform decisions (i.e., strategy).

The key is to determine what the critical measures are. Remember that critical measures are the ones that if they are not what you assume they are will cause you to change what you are doing. The lesson is not to collect data just to be collecting. Only collect those critical data that drive your strategy.

Summary

This chapter has attempted to provide the organization with managerial policies, practices, and philosophies that enhance the ability to create winning strategies that will be implemented effectively. Just as I recommended in the last section, the relationship between these management approaches and improved strategy formulation and implementation have been empirically tested. So no matter what strategic management approach you may ultimately use, implementation of these approaches should improve your chances of achieving the outcome you desire.

Chapter 3: Important Outcomes

The previous chapter provided information on the organizational context that can improve the effect of strategic management on performance. This chapter addresses the characteristics that any effective strategic management system should have. In other words, if the organization truly has an effective strategic management system, these characteristics should be present.

Characteristic 1: Continual Attention to Strategic Issues

A good example of the importance of this point can be seen several years ago in a mid-sized manufacturing firm's strategic management process.

As their strategic planning consultant/facilitator, I worked with the executive group to identify their strategy and the resultant critical assumptions that were underlying the strategy. (A critical assumption is one that if a critical assumption is not true, your actions [strategy] will be forced to change. Thus not all assumptions are necessarily critical.)

One of the elements of their strategy was to utilize their machine tool product as a key component in manufacturing systems that allowed high-volume manufacturers to make changes in their own products without requiring a total retooling of the production line. In effect, their product allowed their customers flexibility in manufacturing high-volume products (flex manufacturing), as opposed to the previous approach, which allowed no flexibility (fixed systems, sometimes referred to as transfer lines). Since transfer lines for high-volume products (e.g., pistons for automotive engines) can cost several hundred million dollars, their technology seemed to provide the basis for a winning product.

However, realizing the key role of assumptions in successful strategic planning, they initially identified that target customers would desire to move to these flex systems to provide useful manufacturing flexibility. Since this was a new manufacturing approach, this could not be assumed to be a fact, and if not true, it would clearly change the strategy the firm pursued to sell the machine tools they possessed. Thus this became a "critical assumption" for the firm.

The strategic management system that they initiated required quarterly meetings to review the strategy and to attempt to disprove their critical assumptions. Notice that the goal was purposely not to "confirm" their assumptions, since this served only to make them feel good, but provided them no new important information to better inform their strategy. This was a result of believing that, as pointed out in the previous chapter, a culture that encourages challenges to critical assumptions is important for strategic management success. All executives were made aware of all the critical assumptions and asked to be on the lookout for any data that were relevant.

At the next quarterly meeting, one of the vice presidents had a report addressing the flexibility critical assumption. He had visited one of the target clients and asked the decision maker directly if they would prefer to buy a flexible system instead of a transfer line. The executive reported that the person answered affirmatively. However, remembering the definition of strategy from chapter 1 (i.e., what one does is more revealing of true beliefs and desires than what one says), the executive further asked the client what kind of system was the most recent system that they had purchased. To the executive's surprise, the client reported they had recently purchased a transfer line, or in essence a fixed system. When pressed, the client answered that even though flex manufacturing made more theoretical sense, from a practical standpoint he did not want to be the first to buy and install a flex line in his company. Because of the enormous cost of such systems, it was too risky, and if it failed, he feared the repercussions of his decision on his career.

This insight did not really change the critical assumption, in that the client indicated that he agreed with the value of flex manufacturing. However, it did provide valuable insight into the decision drivers for purchase of their product. Instead of emphasizing the value of flex in their marketing campaign, they instead focused on obtaining validation data for their flex system that provided confidence in its reliability and effectiveness. Additionally, they developed seminars for target clients using these data to provide more comfort with implementing this new type of manufacturing process. Therefore, by digging deeper into these critical assumptions, valuable knowledge often results that can refine and improve your understanding of what needs to be done.

While this story provides a good example, it doesn't stop there. Approximately six months later, at another one of the quarterly executive strategy review meetings, one of the other vice presidents suggested that the critical assumption with respect to flexible manufacturing was in fact inadequate to support their strategic decisions.

He had returned from a tour of a client's plant. During that tour, he noticed a machine tool product that he had never seen before, and it was at the end of a fixed transfer line system.

Remembering the flex system critical assumption, he inquired about the functionality of the machine located at the end of the transfer line. The answer shocked him! His tour guide reported that that machine allowed the transfer line to be flexible! The VP then realized that instead of the assumption that flex manufacturing is the future of high-volume machining being the appropriate one, the real critical assumption was that *when* flex becomes the preferred manufacturing system for the target market, *our* product solution would be the preferred one!

This realization was huge. It motivated development of an R&D strategy to evaluate alternative ways to achieve flexibility to assure that the firm's approach was best. So what was the value of this continuous attention to strategic issues? Clearly, it refined the firm's understanding of what was important for them to emphasize to achieve their goals. It fundamentally resulted in changes in resource allocation decisions to achieve their goals. In short, it changed their "strategy." (See chapter 6 for actual documentation of this example.)

Discussion of this characteristic sets the stage for the next one, organizational learning.

Characteristic 2: Organizational Learning, Continual Experimentation, and Memory

One of my favorite jokes is the "bear in the woods" story. If you haven't heard it, the joke begins with two friends walking in the woods. Suddenly, in the path before the two friends, a large and very angry bear appears. Upon seeing the bear, both men initially freeze in their tracks, but then one of the men falls to the ground, takes his bulky hiking boots off, and begins to put on a pair of sneakers he had stored in his back pack. The other man is puzzled by this action and nervously tells his friend that it is no use putting on running shoes. Everyone knows that a bear can easily outrun a man, no matter what he wears on his feet. The man on the ground looks up at his friend and calmly says, "I don't need to outrun the bear; I just need to outrun you!"

The application of this story to the above characteristic is that the difference between successful firms and those that are less so is often the comparative amount of good information and understanding they have. As an example, when one firm knows just a little bit more than their competitors about the needs of their target clients, it results in more effective marketing and sales strategies. This ultimately translates into better success in getting a sale and thus into overall competitive advantage. The fact is that no firm is omniscient, but they do not have to be. They just need to know a little more than their competitors. I make this point because often managers are frustrated with the challenge of obtaining information needed to inform better the strategy, since it is not normally a mainline function of their job. They want to decide on what to do and then "just do it." (Or sometimes, folks just want to do something and think about it later.) This story is intended to motivate these individuals to seek useful information and not to be frustrated when definitive answers are not forthcoming.

Thus a characteristic of an effective strategic management system is systematic, continual seeking of knowledge about themselves, their market and clients, and competitors; in other words "learning."

Given the previous points about the reluctance of managers to modify their belief sets, an obvious question becomes how these assumptions that drive decisions (strategy) can effectively change with new information. The answer is a culture of systematic and continual challenge via experimentation.

Many years ago, I was engaged by a software firm to find a better strategy for growing the sales of their products. The problem was stated as follows: The firm sold highly technical software to business clients. These products were sold across the country by trained technical salespeople, all of whom had engineering degrees. To train a new hire in the product took approximately three months and after that approximately six months in the field to become an effective salesperson. To make matters worse, finding technical people who were good salespeople was extremely difficult. Engineers often do not have the interest (or frankly the requisite personality traits) to become salespeople. All of these factors combined to severely limit the sales growth of the firm, even though they believed that they had only begun to scratch the surface of the potential market.

Referring to the value of identifying critical assumptions discussed in chapter 1, I probed to find what the critical assumptions were. While several assumptions were implied, the one that stood out as most important to the current strategy was that the product was so technical that the prospect would need face-to-face explanation of features, benefits, and applications in order to fully appreciate the value of the software. Therefore, trained sales engineers needed to travel to client locations all over the country as the primary means of obtaining sales.

To test this assumption, the firm devised an experiment. They took two non-degreed engineering technicians, gave them some phone sales training, and provided them with telephonic contact information for existing and prospective clients. They also gave them basic training in the software products. They then were turned loose to see what would happen.

The result was revealing. Within six months, these two technicians had sold an amount of software equivalent to that sold by trained engineer salespeople making personal visits. What the management learned was that clients (both existing and prospective) were much more sophisticated in understanding the firm's products and the value they provided than the firm assumed. This allowed these clients to order intelligently. As an added bonus, because the technician salespeople could call many more clients in a day on the telephone than the engineer-trained salespeople could visit in person, they were able to contact clients far more frequently than had been possible previously. This allowed the client to be better served by the firm in terms of addressing interests and questions in a more timely manner. When the customer did have questions that could not be addressed by the technicians, the technicians were trained to obtain the answers and get back to their clients.

This modification of the underlying assumption driving the sales strategy liberated the firm to more effectively and efficiently achieve their growth targets. They were no longer restrained by this flawed assumption. In brief, they learned through active experimentation.

Often firms merely maintain strategies because that is the way things were always done, without continually challenging if the underlying driver of these resource allocation decisions was unchanging. In the previous example, when the firm in question was getting started they had a missionary task. It was absolutely necessary to physically visit prospects to explain the new technology. This approach allowed the firm to succeed, and they maintained that approach because of that fact. However, after a period of time, the technology became more accepted and clients became more knowledgeable. This change allowed for a much more efficient distribution strategy; however, the firm had not had a culture of continual challenge via experimentation to take advantage of the changing environment.

The way business is done can also be driven by industry norms, or so-called "rules of thumb" that are rarely challenged. The opportunity for the firm that continually challenges these rules can be substantial when the rules are proved to be less than completely accurate. A very well-known example of this would be Dell computer. Instead of assuming that people needed to see and touch the computer and be able to ask a trained salesperson for face-to-face assistance in order to buy, Dell changed the business model in the personal computer industry by distributing their products exclusively online instead of through the traditional brick-and-mortar retail stores. This change in assumption about how personal computers could be sold allowed Dell to rapidly become one of the dominant players in the market.

The last aspect of this characteristic is memory. Unfortunately, much of the collective "wisdom" and knowledge accumulated over time in an organization is resident in a few key individuals. Obviously, this represents an enormous risk to the firm. These folks may leave, quit, die, become disabled, or retire. Any of these eventualities could negatively affect the organization's ability to perform.

Another software firm I worked with recently had this problem. The firm was very small, and the main software architect was the only person in the firm who had a working knowledge of the software as well as the market drivers. Unfortunately, he used this knowledge as a lever within the firm to get what he wanted. He closely guarded his knowledge base and refused to cooperate in any experiments to learn more. It took the firm over two years to finally capture the base knowledge he had, thus freeing management up to remove him.

The detrimental effect of this problem could have been minimized if the firm had a systematic formal "memory" mechanism. This requires that critical information for the firm is defined and categorized and that it is written down and captured for access by management. This takes enormous discipline but is a characteristic of successful strategic management systems.

How many times have you had discussions about what was done to address a problem several years ago? Unfortunately, institutional memory is often represented only by incomplete recollections of an individual or individuals in the group. The interpretation of the past event is thus left to the bias of the individual recounting the event and its meaning. How valuable would it be to have a complete record of the event, the context of it, and most importantly, the learning that resulted?

What has surprised me over the years is just how much information can be lost between strategy-related meetings unless these meetings are well documented. People are so busy these days doing multiple tasks that after a very short time what was decided at any particular meeting can be lost. The ability to refer to comprehensive meeting notes is a simple yet powerful way to avoid the time-consuming task of revisiting decisions. It also assists in making certain that everyone remembers the same decisions and the rationale for them. It is an invaluable discipline for any strategic management system.

Consistent with continual attention to strategic issues, this characteristic of successful strategic management systems requires continual challenging of critical assumptions through experimentation and, importantly, systematically recording this knowledge for institutional memory.

Characteristic 3: Articulated Decision-Making Framework

Recalling the definition of strategy, every time a decision is made to commit resources of time or money in an organization, another element in the "pattern of decisions" is added. Because these decisions occur every day in an organization, it is important for the managers (and employees) making these decisions to have a set of criteria to allow the best decisions to be made. Every CEO makes these decisions all the time.

And whether or not the CEO has ever articulated the criteria to himself or others, they are forced to make these decisions. The success or failure of the enterprise depends upon how well this "framework for decision making" fits the firm's capabilities and the environment.

I first confronted this concept as a young sales engineer. I visited one of my clients with the hope of selling them a piece of software to do structural analysis of their products. After making my canned sales pitch, the client engineers told me that the kind of software I was selling was fine but that they just didn't need to use that kind of software very often. However, they had a large sum of money budgeted to develop a project management system. They said that they really needed something like that and that they would use it all the time to track the progress of their product development activity.

They seemed willing to entertain a proposal from our firm to develop such a product. I returned to my company extremely excited. You see, at that time our company was very small, and a significant project like this one would really help us meet the payroll. I relayed the opportunity to the CEO of the firm. This guy was an entrepreneur through and through, and I thought he would really be excited about this opportunity. To my surprise and disappointment, he quickly rejected the idea. He explained to me that while we could probably write this kind of software, our real expertise lay in the area of structural analysis and not project management. If we took on this project, it would take a large percentage of the time of our key software designers. Unfortunately, we would have no competitive advantage in this area. Thus, even though the project might bring needed short-term revenue, it would not be a good use of our resources. The message was to go back out there and find firms that need what we can produce! In other words, spend your time on developing business that is consistent with your strengths.

Initially, I was really disappointed, but over time I began to realize the wisdom of the decision. Had we pursued that opportunity, it would have taken our firm in a direction that did not utilize our advantages and would likely have resulted in lack of focus on our core competencies. This may have resulted in our eventual demise or at least suboptimal performance. Since that time, I have seen lots of firms that were distracted by opportunities that took them away from a consistent focus on what made them successful. I have frequently remarked that what causes firms to fail is often too many opportunities, not too few.

While the CEO in this story was successful in having a framework for decision making, he unfortunately did not articulate it to the rest of the management or employees. As a result, the underlying critical assumptions were never understood and thus could not ever be challenged or modified. Ultimately, this intuitive system of decision making resulted in poor decisions and eventually led the firm to the brink of bankruptcy.

However, any successful strategic management system should result in a set of criteria that will guide every resource allocation decision the firm makes. In my view, this singular characteristic is perhaps the most important and fundamental characteristic, because it is at the heart of what allows an organization to be managed strategically day to day. In fact, I believe it is so central to the strategic management process that I have devoted a separate chapter (4) to introduce and explain the dimensions of just such a decision-making framework for the organization.

In the next section, I will discuss why effective communication of the elements of the framework is another critical element of an optimal strategic management system.

Characteristic 4: Improved Management Communication

The definition of vision that I like best is that a vision represents a "desired future state." It is something to aspire to. One may never achieve the ultimate state, but it provides continual motivation. In the strategic management area, peak effectiveness and efficiency of the firm is only possible to achieve when every employee in the firm makes the same decision as the CEO would if faced with the same alternatives.

The only way to approach this state in any organization is through a commitment to management communication. In the example of the CEO discussed above, he was a brilliant person who didn't (or perhaps couldn't) explain his decision criteria or the underlying assumptions of these criteria to his staff. He was like a lot of brilliant people who had an intuition about what was the correct decision. He was like the person referred to in chapter 1 who can't tell you what exactly he wants or why, but "he knows it when he sees it."

This works as long as the firm is small enough that the CEO is able to be directly involved in every major resource allocation decision. However, as soon as the firm grows large enough to have additional professional management, the system effectiveness breaks down.

The most obvious way the lack of communication negatively affects the organization is that the CEO becomes a significant impediment to getting decisions made in a timely manner. This "hub and spoke" management system eventually gets overloaded, and the firm can only grow so large effectively.

Even if the CEO allows for others on their team to make strategic decisions, without a good understanding of the overall strategy and assumptions, these employees may make decisions that are contrary to the best interests of the firm—not because they want to but because they just don't understand what the CEO wants. These people can only begin to understand what the CEO wants through trial and error.

Referring back to the machine tool company example previously discussed, I was called in initially because the parent company of this firm had requested to see the strategic plan of this company. Even though the firm was several decades old and relatively successful, they had never had a written strategic plan. Like all firms, they had a strategy but had never really written it down nor communicated it. The reason I was selected was because I had worked at another firm with the newly appointed VP of research and development. He was familiar with my approach and apparently felt I could help them.

More important to this person was the fact that he desperately needed to understand the overall firm strategy in order to develop his own plan for R&D. This was a new department set up by management to do applied product development. Unfortunately, without an overall strategy, my friend had no idea what to emphasize. Should he develop totally new products? Which customer needs should they target? Should he emphasize upgrades to current products?

Without clear communication and resultant understanding of the strategy, there was no way my friend could be effective and efficient.

Without clear communication, there is no understanding of what is critical to success. As a result, managers cannot contribute to the refinement of the strategy. They cannot effectively suggest new ideas, because they do not know a priori the criteria for selection of these ideas. This wastes valuable executive time in starting from scratch to evaluate every new idea.

An interesting story about a not-for-profit group exemplifies another value of clear communication of strategy throughout the organization.

A local chamber of commerce wanted to develop a strategy for their organization. To understand the value of communication in this example, it is necessary to understand how this organization worked. The full-time staff consisted of a president, a couple of vice presidents, and approximately twenty employees. The board of directors consisted of a chairperson who served for only one year, a vice chair who automatically took over for the chair in the following fiscal year, and six other board members. All of these folks were community volunteers elected to their positions by the chamber membership.

As the president explained to me, he was extremely frustrated because every year a new chairperson came in and every one of these people had a different idea of what the chamber should focus on. This meant that every year the strategy of the chamber was modified to suit the particular interests of the chair. The result was that the chamber staff was unable to sustain any programs or make significant progress in any meaningful way.

The approach we used involved convening the current board members and staff to develop a strategy for the chamber along with the critical assumptions. Once consensus on this strategy was achieved and approved by the chamber membership at large, the president then made it his sole job to communicate the strategy and its rationale to his staff and all the other constituents of the chamber. Whenever a new chairperson was appointed, the president shared the strategy in detail. Whenever the chair or any other constituent of the chamber suggested a change in direction, the president would bring out his strategy statement and ask if the person had any new insight or data that would contradict any of the critical assumptions. If not, then there was no reason to change the direction or programs being developed. This sent the clear signal of what the organization wanted to achieve and how it was going about achieving the goals. It provided an opportunity for challenge, but with the responsibility to provide disconfirming information.

The president reported that this system allowed him and his staff to focus on the right things and not be annually distracted with a change in direction. Within two years, this chamber was awarded recognition as the top chamber in the United States.

As mentioned earlier, Jack Welsh, well-known former CEO of General Electric, often stated that his only job was to communicate the strategy of GE to all the employees of the firm. Only then could he have any chance of his employees making the correct decisions, consistent with that strategy.

It is clear that any successful strategic management system must be characterized by open communication of strategy throughout the organization that encourages challenge and development of disconfirming data.

Characteristic 5: Integrated/Supportive Functional Plans

A major characteristic of successful strategic management systems is functional plans that support and are consistent with the overall strategy of the firm. A great analogy is a football team. Every player on the team must know how they fit into the success of the whole. The quarterback, or analogously the COO, must know how all the parts work together to achieve the goal of the game and the individual play as it is called. The head coach, or CEO of the team, must have devised the strategy by evaluating the strengths and weaknesses of both his own team and the opponent in designing the overall game plan. As mentioned before, the CEO must adapt the strategy as the game unfolds; thus, like in any organization, the management of the strategy is dynamic.

Using the football analogy in more depth, each position coach could be viewed as the manager of a particular function in the organization. The head coach communicates the basic strategy and approach the team will use—both overall and for a particular game. The position coaches then must devise strategies to best achieve their contribution to the overall success of the team.

A simple example of this can be seen in the University of Cincinnati football team in 2009. The previous coach emphasized the running game to achieve wins. This strategy was supported by the offensive line coach. He recruited the largest, strongest linemen he could find. He was not especially concerned with their foot speed, as they would be asked to create holes for the running backs primarily at the point of attack. The running backs coach looked for large, powerful backs who could accelerate through the hole and overpower defensive linemen at the point of attack.

When the new head coach took over, his strategy was fundamentally different. He wanted to pass the ball and spread the defense to achieve success. This meant that the linemen needed to be lean and mobile. This would allow them to block beyond the line of scrimmage by moving quickly downfield. Running backs needed to be extremely quick and elusive, with pass-catching ability. This would allow them to be evasive once they got beyond the line of scrimmage. All aspects of the team needed to change to be consistent with the new approach. The same is true of organizations that have successful strategic management.

The story in the previous section about the vice president of R&D at the machine tool company provides a perfect example. Before the strategic management system was put in place, he had no direction regarding what to do in order to support the overall strategy of the firm. Once that strategy became clear and well articulated to him, he understood that his role needed to be one of enhancing/modifying existing machines and not attempting to develop totally new products. This drove his own strategy for the R&D department.

Just as the individual football player needs to understand his assignment and role, the individual employee needs also to understand his or her priorities and role. They need to feel that their job, no matter how trivial it may seem, is important to the overall success of the firm.

It is important to point out that an additional value of this coordinated planning process beyond effective and efficient use of resources is the value of empowerment of the individual employee. This results in higher morale of the team and often a willingness to go above and beyond what might otherwise be expected.

A wonderful example of this can be seen in the machine tool firm story. One of the important elements of the firm's strategy was the need to be able to quickly and efficiently change their production line to accommodate changes in the type of machine ordered. This required that the manufacturing VP develop a strategy that allowed tremendous flexibility of work rules on the factory floor. It meant that to be responsive to the flexibility demands of the strategy, he would need highly trained workers who could master multiple manufacturing assignments.

Unfortunately for the manufacturing VP, the firm had a well-entrenched union. As with most unions, this one staunchly resisted allowing individual workers to do more than one job.

They wanted the firm to have to hire more workers to accomplish the desired flexibility, and they did not want any worker to be able to do the work assigned to another. In response to this position, the firm brought the union representative into the strategy discussions. Instead of attempting to enforce their will on the union, they chose to openly discuss their competitive position and why this approach would be critical for the firm's success. They showed the union rep that by being able to handle multiple tasks the union employees would be upgraded in training and thus pay, and their jobs would be as safe as the success of the strategy.

As you might guess, there was considerable skepticism on the part of the union and it took considerable effort on the part of management, but the workers ultimately approved the flexible work rules in the contract. Each union employee became keenly aware of the importance of their job to the firm's overall success and thus to their job security. Their increased training demanded better, more educated recruits that demanded more compensation. The entire factory floor was characterized by workers who cared about their jobs and were willing to do what had to be done to make high-quality products. The pride of the factory floor was a huge advantage to the firm over competitors who had more traditional (i.e., generally more contentious) management/union relations.

The machine tool firm developed goals and action plans down to the individual employee. These plans flowed from the overall corporate strategy, down through each functional unit's plans, and directly to the individual. Each person knew their priorities and tasks, and this provided their managers with actionable criteria for assistance and formal performance evaluation. The result was a coordinated set of actions and consistent resource allocation decisions at all levels in the organization. This approach allowed the firm to grow faster and more profitably than ever before.

Thus a key characteristic to look for is that the firm's strategy is evident in all the actions of the firm at all levels. When new opportunities or resource decision alternatives are presented, the strategic decision framework should be prominently utilized to provide direction. As stated previously, the optimal strategic state of any organization is when any employee or member, when faced with a choice for resource allocation, will consistently make the same decision that the CEO would if faced with the same situation. This can only happen when consistent support strategies are in place and communication is clear and specific throughout.

Characteristic 6: Efficient Environmental Scanning

One thing is indisputable in today's environment, and that is the proliferation of information. We are constantly bombarded with new things every day. Technology is moving so fast that it can be overwhelming to attempt to keep up with everything going on. However, it is critical that organizations continually monitor activities that can impact their business.

To be efficient in this process, the development, refinement, and communication of the critical assumptions that are the foundation for the organization's business model are essential. These critical assumptions can act as a filter for the information we pay attention to, thus eliminating potentially interesting but superfluous material. The example given previously where the machine tool executive was attentive to a new machine tool system was motivated by the awareness of the critical nature of any change in transfer line technology.

The more managers who are aware of the assumptions the better, as this effectively leverages the likelihood that any useful information will be identified. Also, when such information is found and circulated within the organization, there should be immediate recognition of the importance of the information by all other managers. This should initiate discussions as to how to react to the information. Recall that a critical assumption is one that if it is not what you believe it to be would cause you to alter your actions (strategy). Therefore, validation of this kind of information is absolutely of paramount importance to the organization's success.

Characteristic 7: Successor Development

When an effective strategic management system is in place, leadership successors are better prepared to take over. A recent study validated this point specifically with respect to family firms. In this study, it was shown that ownership and leadership succession processes were significantly improved when an effective strategic planning (i.e., management) system was in place. [1]

In my experience in working with family and nonfamily organizations, I have seen this repeatedly. My hypothesis for the reason for this phenomenon is fairly simple. An effective strategic management system embodies all the characteristics discussed above. All of these characteristics imply in-depth understanding and sharing of the factors that drive the organization. Therefore, any manager with significant tenure in the firm should have an intimate appreciation for what makes the organization successful and how and why decisions get made.

Additionally, by having a well-developed system in place, the new leader should be able to assume the leadership position in the organization more simply and effectively than if no system existed. In the case of no system, the individual is faced with

---

1 Mazzola, P., Marchisio, G., & Astrachan, J. (2008). "Strategic planning in family business: A powerful developmental tool for the next generation," *Family Business Review* 2(3): 239–258.

trying to get a grasp of what makes the organization work while initiating a decision-making management system.

Lastly, in an effective strategic management system, all potential successors to the top of the organization should have been actively involved in the strategy creation process. Their abilities, competencies, and deficiencies as strategic decision makers should have been adequately revealed over time. Since the primary role of a general manager/president is strategic management, this provides an exceptional mechanism for selection of the appropriate successor for the organization. Also, the strategic management system should have provided criteria important for the next leader of the organization to possess.

Characteristic 8: Rewards Consistent with Strategic Initiative

The last characteristic is perhaps the most obvious but not necessarily the simplest to achieve. The old adage is you get what you measure and reward. Often salespeople are rewarded for volume of sales based on commissions. They will thus sell what is easiest to sell but not necessarily what may be the most valuable in terms of strategic positioning for the organization. Unless the reward structure is designed to motivate the salesperson consistent with the desired direction of the organization, an obvious disconnect between resources expended and desired results occurs. This is a fairly obvious example of poor alignment of rewards and strategy negatively impacting strategy implementation.

What is less obvious and more difficult to administer is that employees must be rewarded in terms of their contribution to strategy formulation as well. How well do managers follow through on strategic assignments? How professional and complete are strategic reports done? How often does the employee provide valuable disconfirming information, and how well documented and validated is that information?

In today's organizations, where employees are often stretched to their limit just accomplishing their operational responsibilities, asking them to accomplish assignments that do not directly impact sales or costs in the short term is difficult. This is particularly true for organizations with minimal staff resources or with minimal slack in the system that does not allow for outsourcing of "strategic assignments." However, as mentioned previously, if top management does not prioritize these "strategic" activities via measurement and reward, they will not get the attention they deserve. This means that top management must truly value strategic management as just as important to the organization's success as operational management.

To reiterate, what is important is what one does, not what one says. Clearly the reward system of the organization truly reveals those priorities. Therefore, consistency in actions and words is an important characteristic of a successful strategic management system.

Chapter 4: Specific Elements of a Strategic Statement (A Framework for Decision Making)

Now that I have explored some of the realities of strategy and characteristics that are indicators that strategy is being pursued for maximal effect in an organization, the attention shifts to the basic questions that should be answered by any strategy system. Over the years, I have found these elements of a "strategic statement" to represent useful dimensions of a framework for decision making. In other words, these elements are key dimensions that can guide resource allocation decisions. Any good strategic planning process should offer up good answers to the following questions.

In addition, the answers to these questions should form an internally consistent framework. This concept will be further explained at the end of the chapter, once all the individual elements are described.

Question 1: What Are the Organization's Goals and Vision?

The first thing I do as a strategy consultant is to conduct an exercise with the executives involved with strategic planning. I ask each of the managers present to write down on a piece of paper the primary goal of the firm. They are directed to do this privately and not share their information with the other executives, especially the CEO. I then take up the individual pieces of paper and read each goal to the assembled group. Although I have been doing this exercise for some time, in virtually every case the goals listed are not the same. Frankly, the first time I did this, I was very nervous because I had only hypothesized that they would not list the same goal. Over time, I have become less and less concerned.

The point of the exercise is that even though top executives work side by side, sometimes for several years, they normally do not ever talk about the most basic things unless forced to do so by a strategic planning exercise. (Just for fun, try asking your spouse and children to list what they think the primary goal of the family should be. It is interesting and revealing to discuss the different ideas that come out of such an exercise.) The fact is, if everyone has a different view of what the goal of the organization is, it becomes very difficult to work cooperatively to achieve it. Specifically, individual functions are hard pressed to develop functional plans that integrate with other functions to achieve the corporate goal if that goal is not clearly articulated and reinforced with consistent actions.

Strategy consultants and executives implementing a strategic planning process may define what a goal is in slightly different ways. Some are proponents of a single goal. One highly successful executive I know has for thirty years had only one goal for his firm. That goal was to "please the customer." His total focus was on this goal. He believed that if that goal was pursued throughout his organization at every level acceptable sales and profits would follow. Management review meetings did not address sales or profits but instead covered measures of client satisfaction. The result for this private firm was an over 90 percent worldwide market share and extraordinary profitability.

An example of how this goal drove decisions (strategy) of his firm can be seen at the very top of the organization. This CEO had his entire board of directors visit a different customer at every quarterly board meeting. He hired an executive coach vehicle (a converted, customized bus) to transport the board to each location. They then would meet with the top executives of the customer to understand better the client's needs and how they were using the firm's products. One can only imagine the reaction of the clients when this vendor's entire board arrived on the scene. Clearly the customer was impressed with this unprecedented show of concern for their needs.

Other professionals believe in a hierarchy of multiple goals. One firm I have worked with over the years utilizes financial goals as their primary outcome of interest. At the top of the goal hierarchy is profit. Secondary to that goal is sales growth. They prefer to have both if possible but will defer to profitability if additional sales are not profitable. This firm has successfully implemented pursuit of these goals via in-depth budgeting and consistent decisions based on this hierarchy.

Still other professionals believe that the number of goals is not critical but that goals should be more easily understood by employees. For example, they would not like goals of sales and profit, because most employees cannot relate to how they individually can impact these goals. These folks would agree with the CEO of our first example. In other words, establish more actionable goals that assume a relationship with the ultimate outcome desired. In that example, our CEO clearly wanted to achieve outstanding sales and returns but believed that the way to achieve those things was to satisfy the client better than competitors. He believed that each employee could understand what had to be done in their particular role to satisfy the client.

You have no doubt heard somewhere that goals need to achievable, actionable, and measurable. These goals also need to be clearly articulated by management. However, as pointed out previously, this will not be enough if decisions are not made consistent with these goals and actions are not rewarded as a result of employees acting on these goals. As we saw in a previous example, the stated goal for the machinery company was "quality," but everyone knew that the real goal was profit. This caused confusion and cynicism in the employees. In the example of the single-goal proponent above, if employees take initiative based on client satisfaction and it costs significant money, the management had better reward the employees for their actions.

The point here is that no matter how many goals you have or how they are measured, having goals will only be effective if they are consistently used as a basis for making resource allocation decisions. You only really have effective goals if whenever a choice between alternative courses of action is required a simple question is asked: "Which of these alternatives best allows us to achieve our goal or goals?" If this isn't happening on a regular basis, your goals are not useful or meaningful.

Question 2: What Are the Organization's Target Markets?

If the company's goals are well understood and internalized, the next big question becomes what type of client the firm is focused on serving. What clients are most likely to allow the firm to achieve what it wants?

The more specific one can be in identifying the client characteristics, the more precise one can be in serving them. Often, the concept is misunderstood. Managers may feel that by specifying too narrow a definition of the target they will miss other customers that could possibly be served. However, the fact is that just because you target a particular customer doesn't preclude you from serving a broader range of customers. As an example, many years ago Ford Motor Company introduced a car called the Probe. The primary target market for the car was to be young females. The firm attempted to appeal to this market segment via advertising and design. However, a number of males also purchased the car. Obviously, Ford did not deny them the opportunity to purchase the car just because they did not fit the definition of their target market.

There are a couple of things to consider when establishing a target market. First, will the potential market size of the segment allow the organization to fully satisfy the goals that have been laid out? I have participated in many planning meetings where managers identified and persuasively argued for pursuit of other potential market opportunities. When this discussion comes up (and it almost always will at some point) the question needs to be asked "Which market option provides the easiest and most sustainable path for achieving our goals?" Therefore, if you can achieve your goals by staying focused on that segment, it makes little sense to expend resources to establish an additional target. On the other hand, if the current target will not accommodate your goals (or is not anticipated to in the near future), then looking to expand your target may make perfect sense.

The second consideration is the advantage you have in serving the target segment. As we will discuss in more depth later, the reason for choosing a particular market in the first place is that the organization has some advantage over competitors in serving that market. This advantage may have come naturally as the organization grew or may have been planned. In any event, when the firm's many functions are coordinated as recommended in chapter 2, every activity in the firm is designed to meet the needs of that target client. To change the target may mean that the advantage you have worked to obtain may no longer apply in the new market segment. Obviously, one must take into account the cost and risk of modifying that target.

One firm that I have been working with for some time now provides an excellent illustration of the value and importance of defining the target market. This firm is a process machinery company that sells their products worldwide. They utilize a particular mechanical process that is especially cost effective in one kind of application. That application is defined in terms of the particular characteristics of the material being processed. However, it can also be applied to a much broader classification of material, but without the overwhelming advantages.

Initially, the firm made no attempt to focus on the very well-defined segment but instead marketed essentially to all firms that had need for any similar application. They had really not examined in detail the results of their sales, as they did not want to lose any possible opportunity that might be available.

To make a long story short, they did an in-depth analysis of exactly what applications they were successful in selling and for each application the level of profit they earned. What they discovered was that a very specific application specification resulted in significantly higher sales success rates and profitability. They were able to categorize three distinct applications for their product, from most profitable to least.

This recognition allowed them to first ask if these kinds of applications were sufficient to support their sales and profit goals. Once they were confident that for at least the next few years they could satisfy their goals by fully exploiting this segment, they then decided that they should concentrate on "killing the category." Or in other words, focus all their efforts on maximizing penetration of this segment. Along with this recognition, they initiated a development plan to determine what it would take to expand the target market "sweet spot" in the future. The result of this refined target market definition gave guidance and direction to all the supporting functions. Marketing and sales could focus on finding and selling to firms with these applications. R&D could focus on development of products that better served the needs of this type of application. In other words, the entire firm had a sharpened focus. This allowed the firm to be even more successful than before. Interestingly, sales to the less-profitable segments did not significantly diminish, while focus on the most-profitable segments allowed for a higher percentage of total business in the portfolio to come from the target.

The bottom line here is that the better and more refined the organization can be with respect to their target client, the better able the entire organization is to serve that market. Thus any worthwhile strategic management system should result in a very precise definition of the target.

Question 3: What Is the Organization's Competitive Advantage?

Now that the goal or goals of the organization have been clearly articulated and the market target identified that will best allow the organization to succeed, it is time to ask what assets the organization possesses that will allow it to sustain its successful position in that market.

If I have heard it once, I must have heard it a thousand times! When asked about the competitive advantage a firm has, the answer will often be "our people." This drives me crazy. By saying the people working in the organization provide a competitive advantage, the implied assumption is that the people are inherently smarter and more competent than the ones working for the competition. The reality is that there are smart, competent people in every organization. No one organization has the exclusive corner on bright people. No, it is not the people but something else. It could be the system, unique access to resources, management philosophy, or proprietary technology that allows the people to do an outstanding job. This is not to say that people are not important. What it is saying is that people alone are not the advantage. Knowing what the advantage or advantages are is the critical thing.

Unfortunately, it is not always obvious what one's competitive advantages really are. Yet this knowledge is important to have when making decisions about what target markets to pursue.

Let us look at an example of just such a case. Several years ago, I worked with a mid-sized publisher of trade magazines. In the process of developing a strategic plan for the business, the question of competitive advantage was broached. The firm had excellent facilities and years of experience in the publishing industry. Initially, the company management felt that this publishing expertise in the trade publication industry constituted their advantage. Based on this they had ideas of expanding into different industries that had need for trade magazines to achieve their goals of expanding sales and profits.

Upon further examination, two things became apparent. First, trade publication expertise in and of itself was not unique to this firm. Numerous firms had the very same, if not more, experience in creating such magazines. Second, they began to realize that what truly made them so successful in the industry they served was the incredible knowledge and human network that they had established over the years. They knew more about the industry they were in than any other magazine staff. Their connections were extensive and deep; multiple generations deep, in fact. People in the industry they served trusted them and looked to them for information. They determined that their business was not publishing per se, but instead was being a trusted conduit between buyers and sellers in this industry. It therefore was their knowledge and connections in the industry that was their competitive advantage.

This realization reinforced that their target market needed to be the buyers and sellers in this industry. They then assessed the potential of this industry to meet their needs. Once this was accomplished, they looked to expand into different segments of this industry market where they had this invaluable contact and knowledge capital. No longer was the lure of trade magazines in other industries of interest. Clearly, they had no advantage there and thus no reason to pursue these opportunities.

While assessing competitive advantage is essentially an internal exercise, the external dimension is equally important. The external dimension is represented by in-depth knowledge of competitors. It is useful to know their goals and strategies as well as their strengths and weaknesses. After all, you don't have to be perfect; you just need to be better than your competitor (just ask the hiker with the sneakers in his backpack!).

Unfortunately, largely because of the difficulty of obtaining good competitor information, it is often the least well developed strategic information. Too often managers dismiss the competitors with statements implying their lack of competence. Just like the idea that "people" are a competitive advantage, this concept is a very dangerous one.

In a recent *Harvard Business Review* article, the authors reported on a study by McKinsey and Company. Approximately 67 percent of strategic planners felt that understanding competitors and incorporating that knowledge into their strategic decisions was important. However, in a *Marketing Science* article published in 2005, only 10 percent could recall ever having really incorporated such information in their decisions, and fewer than 20 percent expected to do so in the future. Just because this kind of information requires effort does not excuse the fact it is not done. Again, the hiker story is applicable. Obviously, statistics favor those who know at least a little more about their competitors than the competitors know about them.[1]

A good way to address the competitor information problem is to role-play situations with managers playing the role of identified competitors. They can start with assumptions about these organizations and then determine the most logical move the competitor is likely to make. As we discussed in a previous chapter, doing experiments to better understand a competitor's strategy is a good way to get a fix on them over time. As we shall see in the next section, there is a good way to extrapolate competitor moves based on previous actions as well.

It also should provide a mechanism for understanding competitor advantages and predicting their next moves. Lastly, as seen in the example, the system should provide for continual refinement of this knowledge and resultant determination of the appropriate target market for the firm.

Question 4: What Is the Organization's Driving Force?

The driving force is defined as the factor that determines the products and services a company offers and the market or markets that are served. This concept is somewhat subtle and initially difficult to understand. Yet my experience suggests that once fully comprehended, it is one of the most useful and powerful dimensions of strategy. It is useful for motivating strategic decisions internally as well as understanding and predicting competitor moves and reaction to your organization's moves.

---

1 Coyne, K. P., & Horn, J. (2009). "Predicting your competitor's reaction," *Harvard Business Review* 87(4): 90–97.

It is useful to examine how I came to an appreciation of the value of this concept. Many years ago, when a part-time MBA student, I was working full-time for the engineering firm described previously. While taking an introductory marketing course, I became concerned about how our firm was making product and market development decisions. My professor emphasized that the appropriate way to develop products and services was to start by understanding the client's needs. This did not seem to be what we were doing.

Our firm had expertise in dynamic structural analysis. We targeted firms that had problems that could be solved using this technology. This approach resulted in us having clients with mechanical noise problems, ride problems in vehicles, failure problems in mechanical systems, and design problems involving dynamic systems of all types. The common thread in all these applications was that the fundamental cause of the problems that were being experienced was mechanical vibration. We had clients in virtually every industry, but we did not start with their problems as the motivation for offering our products and services. We started with our technology and looked for clients that had problems related to it. In short, we were like a hammer looking for nails to drive.

Around this time, I became aware of a concept developed by Tregoe and Zimmerman.[2] It was an epiphany for me. The authors explained that based on their research there are actually eight legitimate factors that "impact and influence the nature and direction of any organization" other than market needs. Specifically, products offered, technology, production capability, method of sale, method of distribution, natural resources, size/growth, and return/profit represent these possible driving forces. In their experience, every one of the seventy-five firms they studied could be classified as being fundamentally driven

---

2 Tregoe, B., & Zimmerman, J. (1980). *Top Management Strategy: What It Is and How to Make It Work.* New York: Simon and Schuster.

by one of these factors. The takeaway from this article was not a rejection of the marketing concept learned in school but merely a refined understanding. The marketing professor was correct. To be successful, no matter what the driving force is a product or service must ultimately satisfy a need of the target market. It must be "market oriented," but it may not be "market driven." However, how a firm selects the market to target and the products and/or services to offer that market can be different for each firm.

As has been emphasized before, every organization has a driving force, just as they have a strategy, whether they have formally acknowledged it or not. Just like strategy, the key is what the firm does rather than what it says it does. For this reason, the driving force concept is extremely valuable for competitive analysis, as it can be deduced from the organization's observable actions. But before we explore this attribute, it is helpful to give some examples to explain better the concept.

After discovering the concept, I felt much better about my firm's process. Our driving force was technology, and we did not pursue any activity that did not have a fundamental requirement for the application of that technology to solve an important problem. Once we discovered an application for our technology, we assessed the value of that solution to similar clients and the total potential within that industry for our services. Since initially our technology was cutting edge, the primary competitors for our services were often in-house engineering groups as opposed to other firms. We had to assess our relative competitive advantage over these in-house groups. Once satisfied of the value proposition, market size, and our competitive advantage, we actively worked to develop that market opportunity. In short, we were technology driven and market oriented. Recall the discussion in the previous chapter about my boss's decision not to pursue the project management software project; this was a clear example of the use of the driving force concept, albeit intuitive as opposed to analytical.

I also began asking other firm managers about what their driving force was and how it manifested itself. One of the earliest conversations was with the CEO of a mid-sized manufacturer of large ore-hauling trucks. These trucks are huge vehicles that weigh over 170 tons empty and have tires that exceed twenty feet in diameter. They are used to haul ore in large surface strip mines. I explained the concept of driving force to the CEO, and he immediately understood. However, his answer took me by surprise. He explained that the driving force of his firm was the knowledge of how to control electric motors that needed to turn at different rotation rates. It turns out that because of the incredible weight of these trucks, mechanical axles and differentials would add too much weight to the vehicles. This would result in a diminished load capacity, rendering the trucks less than cost effective for the mining customers. The solution was to have five-hundred-horsepower electric motors in each wheel of the truck to drive it, thus eliminating the need for a mechanical differential. When the truck turns, the wheels on the outside must turn at a faster rate than the inside wheels. If this is not precisely controlled, the motors will burn up. His firm specialized in this technology.

I then asked him what he would do if Caterpillar entered the market with a similar product. Without hesitation he replied he would exit the market as quickly (and profitably) as possible. His reason was that if Cat could match his firm's controls ability, his organization would be no match for the competitive advantage of Cat. Cat's reputation for quality and their unmatched service response capability would overwhelm his firm.

The next logical question was what markets he would pursue. He stated they would go to another market where the control technology they possessed was critical to a market need. He went on to say that identifying these new application markets was his major job.

Based on these two examples, you may think that driving force and competitive advantage are the same concept. While they may be similar in some cases, they are not always the same. A good example of that is Procter and Gamble. Based on their product decisions, they would appear to be a market needs driven firm. The specific market definition would be the consumable product needs of consumers. However, their competitive advantage would be their enormous distribution system and marketing expertise.

Another example is the machine tool firm previously discussed. They were an American firm purchased by a Japanese company. The purchasing firm produced a specific machine tool that they "sold" through the subsidiary. The subsidiary therefore had a type of machine with specific attributes that they needed to sell. Thus they were a "products offered" driven firm. However, their competitive advantage was the technology represented in the machine as it related to the needs of the target market.

Some well-known firms provide easily understood examples of different driving forces. "Production capability" firms tend to look for products that can be made with the same equipment or processes. These firms look for economies of scale as a result. Good examples are commodity firms, such as paper manufacturers. A well-known "method of distribution" firm would be Dell computers, while Avon and the famous Avon lady could be considered a "method of sale" driven firm. Arm and Hammer would be a "natural resources" driven firm, as they seem to have an unlimited supply of baking soda, upon which they base all of their products. Lastly, size/growth could be the driving force of a conglomerate like General Electric.

From a competitive analysis perspective, a good example of the use of the driving force concept is the acquisition of Hughes Aircraft by General Motors several years ago. I recall the reaction in the *Wall Street Journal* at the time that Hughes' competitors should be concerned, as GM could provide significant additional resources to fuel Hughes' expansion of market share. However, the history of GM suggested that they were fundamentally interested in producing rubber-tired vehicles. Their actions clearly suggested they were a "product driven" firm. They showed nothing to suggest branching into aerospace. So why buy an aerospace firm if not for diversification? The most likely reason was a desire to obtain aerospace technology to make lighter-weight cars so as to improve fuel economy—a desirable characteristic of rubber-tired vehicles with rising fossil fuel prices.

This assessment could have fueled an opportunity on the part of Hughes' competitors. If in fact this was GM's intent, there would likely be dissatisfied Hughes employees who had specifically wanted to be part of an aerospace firm; good people who would have no interest in building cars. These competitors could have easily tested this assumption by pursuing top Hughes' managers. They also could have launched aggressive marketing campaigns to attempt to take share from a distracted Hughes, as opposed to taking defensive positions fearing an aggressive onslaught from Hughes.

About two years after the takeover, an interesting GM advertisement on TV seemed to validate this assumption. The TV ad showed an experimental solar-powered car driving across the desert. The car had been developed by the Hughes division of GM. What a surprise.

The point of all this is that driving force is a highly useful concept to describe the strategy of an organization. As with all the dimensions so far addressed, it is interdependent. In short, to reach a goal, one must have selected a target market consistent with the competitive advantages of the firm and the fundamental driving force.

Question 5: What Is the Organization's Growth Direction?

This question is addressed very simply by a two-by-two matrix of products/services and clients/markets. There are essentially four different options for growing the organization. New products/services to new clients/markets is clearly the most difficult option to accomplish, while current products/services to current clients/markets is the most conservative.

The fundamental answer to this question simply addresses where one believes the organization should put the most emphasis to achieve its goals. It does not mean that the firm cannot operate in more than one quadrant of the matrix, but it does require that all the resources of the firm be mobilized and coordinated to attack effectively only one of the quadrants.

This information, along with the answers to the other questions posed previously, serves to further define the strategy of the organization. The rationale for the selection of the appropriate quadrant can come from many sources. The competitive advantage of the firm may provide the opportunity to enter a new market where this advantage can provide superior returns. An example of this would be Procter and Gamble's entry into cosmetics. The competitive advantage of P&G includes massive distribution capability and advertising clout, which allowed it to almost immediately overcome entry barriers of this industry and introduce a new distribution model at the same time. This changed the business model for the industry from primarily department store and boutique distribution to grocery stores and immediately gave P&G a great advantage. Since its driving force was consistent with a consumable product and it apparently met the sales and profit goals of the firm, the growth direction quadrant of new products to existing customers represented by this move made sense.

The fact is that the growth direction may change often, as opportunities and challenges present themselves. In addition, as pointed out in the P&G example, whatever that direction is, it must be consistent with the other dimensions of the firm's strategy to be successful.

As mentioned earlier, an observation I have made over the years is that one of the biggest problems firms have is to have too many opportunities as opposed to too few. When multiple opportunities present themselves, great discipline is required to keep from being distracted. Firms can dissipate energy, resources, and focus when they are pulled by the siren song of these new opportunities. That is why formally restricting the organization's emphasis to only one growth direction can help provide important focus to the activities throughout the firm.

This is particularly important to small firms that have some initial success and, as a result, attract people with ideas to take advantage of that success. If not careful, the management may take its eyes off the ball of their core business, not be successful in the new opportunity, and lose their position in the core business as well. Many of the businesses I have been involved with have difficulty successfully focusing all their efforts on one growth direction, let alone two.

Question 6: What Is the Organization's Generic Competitive Strategy?

In 1980, Michael Porter turned industrial organization economic principles upside down and introduced his now famous five forces model for assessing the profit potential of industries.[3] Along with this model, he introduced his four generic competitive strategies.

1. Low Cost
2. Differentiation
3. Focus-Low Cost
4. Focus-Differentiation

While there have been many challenges and modifications to this framework over the intervening years, the concept has largely met the test of time. I include it as an important question to be addressed by strategists because of its value for providing yet another dimension to inform resource allocation decisions (or strategy). The four possible generic strategies represent the fundamental culture of the firm as much as anything.

An example of what I mean by this is found in a mid-sized manufacturing firm I have worked with for many years. The culture of this firm is one of going the extra mile for their customers. They do not compete on price as much as on reliability and service after the sale. They sell the highest-quality product in their industry and are proud of it. They have had opportunities to sell a low-cost product but have resisted. They clearly have a differentiation culture. All of their people in all of their functional areas are geared to this differentiation culture. To make a decision to move in a direction of low-cost producer would require enormous systemic change. Unless the environment requires this kind of change for survival, the organization simply is not capable of making such a change.

Thus I suggest that any framework of strategic decision making must include this basic dimension.

---

3   Porter, M. E. (1980). *Competitive Strategy: Techniques for Analyzing Industries and Competitors.* New York: The Free Press.

Summary

My experience suggests that the answers to the six questions posed above, along with the critical assumptions that back them up, provide a complete and effective "framework for strategic decision making." Taken together, the answers to these six questions form what I call the "strategic statement" for the organization. (Interestingly, this framework can be and has been effectively applied to organizational entities like R&D departments within the larger firm as well to guide behavior in a "strategic" path.)

The environment facing today's executives and their firms is so volatile and unpredictable that attempting to develop stable and unchanging plans is not feasible. What is required is the ability to react to various situations using a set of interdependent and related criteria. As discussed in chapter 2, these elements must be continually challenged by and communicated to the entire organization and a system established to keep track of the knowledge gained in the process.

Whenever a resource allocation decision needs to be made, all of these elements should be considered, and taken together they should make sense. If the policies and characteristics described in chapter 2 are in place, alternatives can be assessed quickly and effectively, as everyone should understand the organization's decision criteria and their rationale. This eliminates the inefficiencies associated with trying to make a decision when everyone involved has a different idea of what is important. As important as efficient evaluation of alternatives is the generation of these ideas in the first place. If employees understand the criteria, they are in a much better position to generate ideas to achieve better the goals of the organization and then to prepare relevant information that supports their suggestions. This further enhances the ability to optimize the assets of the organization.

What often happens in organizations that have not taken the time to elaborate the criteria for strategic decisions is that every time a decision has to be made, the management team must start over to evaluate the merits. Over time, the preferences of the chief executive making final decisions may be deduced by the rest of the management team. However, this is extremely inefficient and frankly wastes the valuable time of all involved. It also does not provide any mechanism to discover flaws in the logic of the chief executive's decision model. Clearly this situation results in ineffective and inefficient decision making.

In summary, to achieve its goals a firm should be operating in the best possible market segment, utilizing sustainable competitive advantages consistent with its driving force and generic competitive strategy. It should not move to new products/services or new markets unless these same dimensions support that move. Further, the critical assumptions underlying this framework should continually be challenged and tested so that the organization is always learning.

What follows in the next chapter is a description of a simple process model that can be used to manage any organization's strategy.

Chapter 5: A Simplified Strategic Management System

Assuming that the maximal policies and managerial philosophies discussed in the previous chapters are in place, the following simple strategic management system can be effectively implemented. While the management process shown below in figure 1 can be used for a brand-new fledgling enterprise, the presumption is that most organizations that will employ this system will be "going concerns." The description that follows is based on introducing the system in such an organization. Obviously, the system can be used for a totally new, start-up organization, but in that case step 1 described below would be eliminated and step 2 would be the first one.

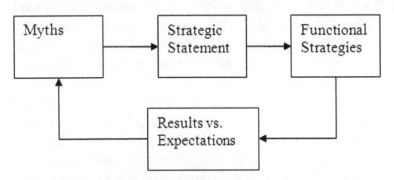

Figure 1: Strategic Management System

Involvement

Often the question becomes who should be involved in strategic management discussions. The answer is different for each organization. For not-for-profits, I recommend the volunteer board of trustees/directors and the CEO and top functional managers of the organization. For-profit firms generally have at least the top functional managers and the CEO. In both cases, it is valuable to have an unbiased professional facilitator to get the process started. However, any such facilitator should be working to make the group self-sufficient in such deliberations, as this strategic management system should become an integral part of the management of the firm. Just as operational management meetings are generally not facilitated by outsiders, the goal should be to learn how to manage strategically without outside facilitation.

The following steps are described without examples, as the next chapter will provide extensive actual examples of this process and its variations.

Step 1

As described in chapter 1, being a "going concern" implies that whether articulated or not, the organization is currently pursuing a "strategy." Thus the first step in initiating the process is to describe the six elements of the current strategic statement based on the best abilities of the management to reflect the actual decisions that are being made. This step is represented by the "Strategic Statement" block shown in figure 1. The important part of this step is to be as objective as possible when describing the strategic elements. They must represent what is *actually* going on and not what is hoped to be going on. The story of the company whose employees stated initially that quality was the number one goal of the firm and then, with the help of some facilitation, agreed that sales and profit goals were really the main goal of the firm provides a good example of what this means. It is critically important that people be open and honest and allowed to challenge the results of this step. The best way to gain consensus is to utilize examples of what actually was done that can validate the answers to these questions. As previously pointed out, the process is basically worthless without objectivity.

Step 2

Once the elements are agreed upon by those involved in the process, the next step is to develop a set of assumptions that are implied based on what has been articulated in the strategic statement. In other words, if the strategic statement is correct, what must we believe to be true that would logically support the strategy statement just developed? Categories of assumptions include what we believe to be true about the industry in which the organization competes, the competitors, the markets and clients served, and finally the organization's strengths, weaknesses, opportunities, and threats. This is represented by the "Myths" block in figure 1.

Note that most strategic planning processes start with a traditional "SWOT" analysis (i.e., *S*trengths, *W*eaknesses, *O*pportunities, and *T*hreats) as a first step. The rationale is that such an assessment provides the foundation for development of the strategy. My experience suggests that such an exercise rarely results in any meaningful insight. Not only that, but most of the items on such lists tend to be irrelevant or not critical to the organization. I do not mean to imply that such an exercise is worthless. However, by focusing on underlying assumptions of current actions, the relevant SWOT elements are naturally revealed. This makes it far more efficient to explore the elements that truly affect the organization.

By starting with the items that are directly related to the existing strategy statement, irrelevant items are automatically eliminated from concern. This allows concentrated evaluation of those assumptions in order to identify the ones that are truly critical to the strategy being employed. Critical assumptions are defined as those that (1) are not certain (or do not represent actual facts) and (2) if not correct, would cause the strategy to be modified to better pursue the goals of the organization.

These critical assumptions make up the lifeblood of the process and require significant attention. Once the critical assumptions have been identified, they can be examined for their face validity. In other words, people may not really agree that the assumption implied from the strategic statement is actually true. If it is the consensus of the group that the critical assumption is not valid, then it should be modified to align better with the group's model of reality. Clearly, if a critical assumption is not felt to be accurate, by the very definition of "critical assumption," some aspect of the strategic statement would need to be changed. This then constitutes the next step in the process: revising the strategic statement to reflect what the organization intends based on what they really believe to be true. The organization must be made to realize that this statement is a "snapshot in time," and as such it will be continually revisited and potentially revised at any time. It becomes the basis for all organizational learning through the continual challenge of the critical assumptions.

Step 3

Once the strategic statement is completed to the satisfaction of the group and/or the chief executive, it can be communicated to the various departments as a basis for the development of their own functional plans. The "Functional Strategies" block in figure 1 represents this step. As such, this strategic statement is the foundation for the yearly operational plans of all units in the organization.

Step 4

Concurrent with development of operational plans is the initiation of testing the critical assumptions for their validity. Individual executive team members will be assigned to gather more information with respect to a particular critical assumption. They essentially "own" this assumption. Their assignment is to find out as much as they can about the assumption and prove it false if at all possible. At some regular time intervals, the executive team will convene in a strategy meeting to report on the status of these investigations and to refine the strategic statement as necessary. This part of the process is where organizational learning occurs.

The process continues indefinitely in this manner. If done diligently and in accordance with the accountability required of a successful system, the organization will be in an ever-growing learning mode. This allows for what I call a "strategic continuous improvement" cycle.

What follows in the next chapter are very different examples of the application of this model to three very different organizations. As you will see, each organization started with the basic model based on their buy-in to the underlying philosophy upon which it is built. However, each utilized the process and refined it to fit their individual culture and needs. By describing these cases, it is hoped that the reader will gain an appreciation for the value of the process as well as the confidence to modify it as they see fit. After all, the fundamental value of any strategic management system is to affect real behavior in a positive way. That is the absolute measure of the value of such a system.

Chapter 6: Real Examples

As described in the introduction, "Managers modify basic strategy processes and tools to fit best their specific organization, culture, external environment, personal preferences, managerial philosophies, and styles." [1] This is certainly true for the basic process model and philosophies described in the previous chapters.

The objective of this chapter is to provide some very different examples of how real organizations have used this model to improve their performance. Obviously, each one approached the management of their strategy in a very different way, but top management of all three organizations shared the fundamental philosophy described in this book and upon which the model is based.

In order to make the information contained in this chapter as valuable as possible, each example will begin with a brief description of the organization and the rationale for pursuing a different approach to strategically managing each of them. Following this initial setup, a description of the process followed will be presented. Examples of actual documents the organization used to summarize their strategic position are included so the reader can understand better the results of each process. Finally, the impact of the process on the firm will be

1   Knott, P. (2008). "Strategy tools: Who really uses them?" *Journal of Business Strategy* 29(5): 26–31.

explained in a "commentary" section. What will not be shared is financial information on these organizations unless divulged by the chief executive in the impact section described below.

These "commentary" sections are particularly interesting, as the top managers who implemented the process for their organizations have graciously consented to comment on the value of the strategic management process from their own perspectives. They have been encouraged to be as objective as possible so as to provide the reader with the best possible information, although I have not required that they discuss specific financial information. In addition, they have agreed to edit my description of the process to make sure it is an accurate representation. Obviously, as the author of the process and facilitator of the work described, my assessment would potentially be biased. Thus the inclusion of the actual persons who had to implement the process as evaluators provides a large measure of objectivity.

A final word before beginning is that the three cases that follow were chosen based on the following criteria: First and most obvious, they had to be organizations that I had personally facilitated. Second, I wanted organizations that had taken significantly different paths as the process moved forward to show different ways to use the model. Third, I wanted both for-profit and not-for-profit organizations represented. Fourth, the implementation of the strategic management approach had to have been used for a long enough period of time to allow for assessment of the value. Finally, the top managers involved had to agree to share their process and results as well as be willing to write a commentary on their assessment for inclusion in the book.

Example 1: Makino, Inc., North American Subsidiary of Makino Milling Machine Co. of Japan

Background

The Makino Milling Machine Company, Tokyo, Japan, bought a controlling interest in the LeBlond Machine Tool Company of Cincinnati, Ohio, in 1981. The company then became known as the LeBlond Makino Machine Tool Company. By the mid 1990s, Makino Milling Machine Company had acquired all of the shares, the name had been changed, and the company was known as Makino, Inc., subsidiary of Makino Milling Machine Company. The original firm was founded in Cincinnati, Ohio, in the late 1800s by R. K. LeBlond. From its founding until 1981, the primary product of the R. K. LeBlond Machine Tool Company was lathes. After Makino's investment, machining centers and other Makino-developed products began to be produced and sold by the acquired firm.

In 1989, a new plant was built in Mason, Ohio, to meet the current and future needs of the business. This plant replaced the seventy-two-year-old plant that had housed the company successfully for those many years. A second phase of expansion was described in a 1998 *Cincinnati Business Courier* article that stated that "it became obvious that the exacting specifications, extreme temperature requirements and the necessity for 'clean' environments, coupled with the size and weight of the lathes (and other machine tools), would force LeBlond to move. Modern manufacturing standards could no longer be maintained in a 72-year-old facility."

By 1990, the combination of a new facility, new products, and new ownership weighed heavily on the president of the firm, Mr. Donald Bowers. Even though the firm had survived and at times thrived for over a hundred years, the firm had no current strategic plan for the future of the new organization. About this time, a new research and development activity was initiated and a vice president of R&D was hired. This new VP wanted some direction for his department that was consistent with the firm's strategy. Interestingly, the decision to have some product development in the Cincinnati facility revealed discordant agendas from different groups in the firm, both domestic and foreign. Some people felt the new R&D department should develop new products, while others felt it should focus on refinements of existing products. Given the need to clarify direction for this new activity and the historically cyclical nature of the machine tool business, Mr. Bowers knew that it was imperative that a clear strategy be established and communicated to the rest of the organization so that everyone could work together effectively.

Group Selected to Develop the Strategic Management System

The initial group selected to develop the strategy process to be used by the firm consisted of the president and the vice presidents of the three operating divisions or units making up the firm. In addition to these people, the VP of administration, the controller, the VP of manufacturing, and the VP of R&D were also included. (As discussed previously, it is absolutely critical to have these meetings captured in well-written notes. The VP of administration was assigned this important task. Later on in this section, selected samples of these meeting notes are included to provide a feel for the detail required and the value of these notes for subsequent strategic management.) In addition, as specific information was needed by the group other individuals were invited to attend from time to time.

In order to understand the process, it is helpful to understand something about the operational units. The largest division was the Production Machinery Division. This division was responsible for manufacture and sales of the large horizontal milling machines designed originally by Makino Japan. This division was not charged with developing new machines to address U.S. customers but instead was asked to modify designs (as necessary), to develop the machining processes and customized tooling and to sell "turnkey" solutions to produce high-volume automotive parts.

The second largest division was the Die Mold Division. Once again, the charge did not include new development but instead manufacturing, marketing, and selling the die mold machines that had been developed by Makino Japan.

The Regal Lathe Division was the smallest of the three divisions but the most profitable. This division's primary task was to sell parts and service for the hundreds and hundreds of LeBlond lathes that had been sold over the previous decades. As a spare parts business, this division was a high-margin cash generator whose business would eventually go away as the LeBlond lathes would be continually retired from service with no new replacements.

The Process

The process began with an initial three-day intensive workshop with the executive group. The program started with a tutorial that presented the approach described in this book. Following this presentation, the group determined that it was more beneficial for managing the business to focus strategizing at the divisional level and not the corporate level. This decision was made because of the fact that each division had different products, services, and customers. The corporate goal then became one of maximizing the performance of each of the operating divisions independently as the most direct way to maximize performance of the corporation as a whole.

It was agreed that the strategic management system would consist of the following process (taken from original documents) for each division:

Strategic Planning Process

    I.   Define strategic statement (SS)
    II. Define the critical assumptions that support the SS
    III. Analyze major competitors' strategies
    IV. Develop functional strategies (departmental objectives)

Operational Planning Process

    V.   Use departmental objectives to develop department actions
    VI. Schedule key individual tasks
    VII. Prepare periodic business plans

How this process worked was as follows. Items I–IV above were reviewed on a quarterly basis by the executive team for each division, led by the CEO, Donald Bowers. As the sample notes from some of these meetings will show, strategic assignments were made and managers held accountable for the execution of these assignments by the CEO. This process of challenge and learning was continual. Everyone understood that they effectively would never finish the process, as it would be continually changing and evolving.

The operational planning process shown was initiated in the fourth quarter of every year by divisional management to develop the yearly plan and budget based on the functional strategies developed in the strategic plan. As will be shown, the strategy was translated all the way down to an individual level through the use of key individual tasks, or KITs. Thus each person in the firm (other than the union shop floor and some administrative support personnel) had a yearly plan that was directly tied in with the priorities outlined in the strategy and fully coordinated with others in the organization.

The group then worked to develop the strategic statements and related critical assumptions for each of the three divisions. Once this initial work was completed, assignments to test the assumptions were made and the quarterly strategic meetings were scheduled. Every three months, each division had a separate day devoted to reviewing the strategic statements and the critical assumptions with the objective being to hone and refine the strategy. Additional executives of each division were included in these meetings to provide necessary information.

By managing this process, Donald Bowers quickly recognized that the direction of these meetings and the decisions made in them provided him with the best way to strategically manage the firm. (This is my belief; Mr. Bowers may state his own belief in the impact segment below.)

Examples of Output

What follows are copies of the actual notes describing an early quarterly meeting of the Production Machinery Division. These documents are included in their entirety to provide a complete view of what level of detail and specificity was necessary to affect behavior. Obviously, the time of these meetings was sufficiently long ago that the actual contents of the notes do not reveal any current competitive positioning for Makino. However, the opportunity to look inside the detailed strategic thinking of such a firm is hoped to be of significant value to the reader.

The Production Machinery Division meeting note includes the complete divisional strategic statement, critical assumptions, and the functional strategies the division intends to follow. Also, a KIT for a particular individual employee in the division is provided to show what these looked like. Last is a report that was done to examine a specific critical assumption—assumption 2. This report was delivered to the strategy group per an earlier assignment. This report is particularly significant in that you will notice that the actual assumption (2) is modified in the meeting notes provided. Looking at the dates, it is apparent that a change was made in this assumption between delivery of the report and the meeting. This is the actual documentation of the example provided in chapter 3, where the critical assumption was modified based on the observation of a key executive. Refer to the description of this situation under characteristic 1 in chapter 3.

LEBLOND MAKINO
MACHINE TOOL COMPANY

**DEPARTMENTAL
CORRESPONDENCE**

DATE: February 20, 1992

TO: --------------------------   S. Barton   D. Lane
                                        D. Bowers   D. LeBlond
FROM: Gary Donovan   T. Clark   K. Mayak
                                        W. Howard   K. Namba
SUBJECT: STRATEGIC PLANNING   J. Knobeloch   S. Ogawa
         PRODUCTION MACHINERY DIVISION

The attached are updated documents from our February meeting to be
inserted into your Strategic Planning binders. We reconsidered our
goals and objectives for the Production Machinery Division and made
revisions. The next meeting is scheduled for April 15, 1992. We
will follow the same schedule as before.

The assignments for the meeting are a continued review of earlier
assignments, plus the following:

NEW ASSIGNMENTS

1. GWK -   Form a committee to develope an alternative
            terminology for "Turnkeys and systems".

2. DDB -   Will take Roman -IV ANALYZE MAJOR COMPETITORS
            STRATEGIES and examine Mazak.

3. WGH - In support of Critical Assumption #2, need to
            continue our attempts to get inside Nissan.

4. WGH -   Develop a market segment measurement and technical
            report on expanded machining center applications in
            automotive parts manufacturing.

         - Provide status report on the Cummins Seymour and
            Ford engine projects.

         - Answer the following questions:

            a. What types of flex equipment will be used in
                automotive?

            b. What types of flex equipment will be used by
                automotive application?

            c. What automotive application is our target?

86

5. TFC - Review all Critical Assumptions for redundancy and vagueness. Draft revisions as necessary.

6. KWM - Need to establish the actual costs incurred against the Saturn P.O.

   - Determine how we are tracking the direct costs of Application Engineering, Service Engineering, and Systems Engineering.

   - Re-cost our actual overhead costs.

   - Analyze the MT charges vs. work performed.

7. GWK - Continue to analyze the scope and number of design changes at Saturn and use this data to further refine the model to measure the effectiveness of flex for Saturn.

8. GWK - Determine why a medium-volume manufacturer buys or values turnkeys.

9. DDL - Prepare a micro-forecast of A55 Horizontal Machining Center competitors by size to test the total market as part of this study in support of Critical Assumption #14.

GLD:dkd.1122
enclosure

87

PRODUCTION MACHINERY DIVISION

I. STRATEGIC STATEMENT

    A. GOALS AND OBJECTIVES

        1. Attain a reputation as a leader in quality and technology in targeted segments of Machine Tool Industry.

        2. Maintain profitability - consistent profitability (targeted at 8%-12% on sales and to reduce our debt).

        3. Growth is desired within target markets; where necessary to support the objectives of profitability; to maintain our reputation as an industry leader; and to create an environment that fosters development of our human resources.

    B. GROWTH DIRECTION

        1. Growth will be pursued in high technology, value-added products and services in focused niches.

        2. Continuous improvement of current products.

        3. Improve the efficiency/skills of present employees.

            a. Motivate or energize the organization.

            b. Broaden our employees' scope.

        4. Shrink or manage the phase-out of low technology products.

        5. While leveraging Makino's technology, we should expand and grow or increase control in areas where LM has an opportunity for contributing value.

            a. Turnkeys
            b. Engineered Systems
            c. Other Value added Services

PRODUCTION MACHINERY DIVISION

C. COMPETITIVE ADVANTAGES

   1. Industry Leading Quality Product:

      a. Reliability
      b. Accuracy

   2. Strong Customer Service Capability:

      a. Turnkeys
      b. Engineered Systems

   3. World-class manufacturing
      facilities:

      a. Environmentally controlled
      b. Based in U.S.

   4. Substantive Image - Know How

   5. Leading Technology:

      a. Accuracy
      b. Hi-Speed
      c. Cell Hardware/Software

D. DRIVING FORCE

   1. Products Offered

E. GENERIC STRATEGY

   1. Focused Differentiation

1/92

89

II. CRITICAL ASSUMPTIONS

CRITICAL ASSUMPTION #1

"Our customers wanted and will continue to want the value-added services provided by LeBlond Makino. They are willing to pay the necessary premium for them."

CRITICAL ASSUMPTION #2

"A, there will be a migration from transfer lines to flexible cells and systems; and B, that LM products and reasonable derivatives will provide a cost-effective solution in this migration."

Additionally, we need to determine:

1. Pace of migration (growth of served market).

2. How much premium will customer pay for this flexibility?

CRITICAL ASSUMPTION #3

"The Voluntary Restraining Agreement will have no impact on LeBlond Makino strategy, but will impact the risk involved in executing that strategy."

CRITICAL ASSUMPTION #4

"The strategic plans of our vendors and suppliers will not impact our strategies."

CRITICAL ASSUMPTION #5

"FMS will continue to be a viable manufacturing technology."

CRITICAL ASSUMPTION #6

"Material substitutes won't affect the metal-cutting market."

CRITICAL ASSUMPTION #7

"The metal-cutting market will not significantly migrate to or from North and South America." There will be a more significant increase in manufacturing activities in Latin America.

CRITICAL ASSUMPTION #8

"Makino Tokyo will continue to develop the required technology to support LeBlond Makino's competitive advantage."

1/92

CRITICAL ASSUMPTION #9

"LeBlond Makino will be able to finance the development of unique market-driven products and features."

CRITICAL ASSUMPTION #10

"LeBlond Makino can recruit, train, and retain the technical manpower necessary to support it."

CRITICAL ASSUMPTION #11

"LeBlond Makino can achieve Manufacturing efficiency and competitive productivity."

CRITICAL ASSUMPTION #12

"The LM system at Saturn is a financial success."

CRITICAL ASSUMPTION #13

"High-volume and low-volume market segments react differently in regards to buying turnkeys."

CRITICAL ASSUMPTION #14

"Customers and target markets can support LeBlond Makino operations."

CRITICAL ASSUMPTION #15

"LeBlond Makino can eliminate debt."

CRITICAL ASSUMPTION #16

"A two million dollar investment in Management Information Systems is sufficient, but necessary to execute this strategy."

CRITICAL ASSUMPTION #17

"Local production is required for success in the target markets."

CRITICAL ASSUMPTION #18:

"MT views LeBlond Makino as a viable entity who should profit in an environment of reasonable, operational independence."

1/92

91

III. <u>STRATEGIC MARKET TARGETS</u>

MID-VOLUME (GREATER THAN 75,000 PER YEAR;
LESS THAN OR EQUAL TO 500,000 PER YEAR)

LOW TO MID FLEX APPLICATIONS

(LOW TO HIGH FLEX NEEDS)

<u>CHARACTERISTICS</u>:

- EMERGING

- VALUE ADDED OPPORTUNITY

    - MMC ENGINEERING

    - TURNKEY

    - SERVICE CONTRACTS
      (INCLUDING PREVENTATIVE MAINTENANCE)

    - PILOT PRODUCTION

    - TRAINING AND CONTRACT MANAGEMENT

- COMPETITIVE PRESSURE FROM TRANSFER AND CNC

- PREMIUM AND DEMAND ON UPTIME

- LOCAL (U.S.) SUPPORT

- NEW TECHNOLOGY EQUALS GREATER RISK EQUALS
  GREATER VALUE ON DEPENDABILITY, SUCCESS,
  QUALITY, RELIABILITY

1/92

V. FUNCTIONAL STRATEGIES

A. DEVELOP TARGET MARKET

1. Sponsor/produce "Flex seminars" with "expert" lecturers and panelists from Academic, Society of Manufacturing Engineers, Industry and LeBlond Makino.

B. PRODUCT PROMOTION STRATEGIES

1. Promote LeBlond Makino's image as stated.

   - A Reliable Strategic Partner

   - An Experienced Turnkey Vendor with leading edge metal cutting technology

   - Hi-Quality (accuracy/reliability) Machine Tool Builder with 5 years of experience in providing turnkey solutions to mid-volume (75,000 to 500,000 units per year) prismatic part machining problems.

2. Educate the market that LeBlond is the solution to their manufacturing problems. (example: Flex Seminars with expert panelists.)

C. PRICING STRATEGIES

1. Be Premium Priced While Delivering Competitive Value.

   - Un-bundle Turnkey Services and Invoice upon Milestone Completion.

   - Get Paid for all Products/Services.

D. SALES AND DISTRIBUTION STRATEGIES

1. Establish and Maintain a Highly Technical/Consultative Sales Force.

2. Be Highly Focused on Target Accounts.

1/92

PRODUCTION MACHINERY DIVISION

E. **MARKET INTELLIGENCE STRATEGIES**

1. Initiate and sustain a comprehensive market and competitor intelligence activity.

2. Maintain the Strategic Statement and "Myths".

F. **APPLICATION ENGINEERING STRATEGIES**

1. Maintain a profitable value-added product with uncompromising value to the customer.

2. Minimize risk by limiting turnkey installations to those cells/systems where LeBlond Makino has all of the critical and the majority of the machinery.

3. Assure quality and reputation by a disciplined post-audit of customer's performance.

4. Develop and maintain leading edge metal cutting technology.

G. **SYSTEMS ENGINEERING STRATEGIES**

1. Maintain a profitable value-added product with uncompromising value to the customer.

2. Minimize risk by limiting (turnkey) installations to those cells/systems where LeBlond Makino has all of the critical and the majority of machinery.

3. Assure quality and reputation by a disciplined post-audit of customer's performance.

H. **PRODUCT DEVELOPMENT STRATEGIES**
    (HARDWARE & SOFTWARE)

1. LeBlond Makino will have a product development activity that leverages and complements Makino Tokyo's activities as required to serve the target market.

1/92

94

PRODUCTION MACHINERY DIVISION

K. CUSTOMER TRAINING STRATEGIES

1. Create a profitable value-added product with uncompromising value to the customer (except for a 1-year warranty package).

2. Minimize risk by limiting customer training to those installations where LeBlond Makino has all of the critical and the majority of the machinery.

3. Assure quality and reputation by a disciplined post-audit of customer's performance.

4. Pro-actively develop programs for extended training (prior to shipment, at installation and start-up, and post acceptance remedial or advanced training).

5. Sponsor/produce "Seminars" with "expert" lecturers and panelists from Academia, Society of Manufacturing Engineers, Industry, and LeBlond Makino.

L. PERSONNEL RECRUITMENT AND DEVELOPMENT

1. Professionally recruit well-educated, hi-potential engineering graduates from a "close" network of universities who "cooperate" in "flex" technologies.

2. Recruit well-educated, 2-year graduates in technology programs for product support.

3. Provide a challenging work environment that stimulates and professionally rewards employees.

4. Pay a competitive salary and provide a responsive benefit package and "flex rules" that are required to attract and retain exceptional people.

M. MANAGEMENT INFORMATION SYSTEMS STRATEGY

1. Develop and maintain a flexible, responsive, and efficient Management Information System that provides essential management information.

1/92

95

IV. ANALYZE MAJOR COMPETITORS' STRATEGIES

   -- In process --

1/92

SCHEDULE OF KEY INDIVIDUAL TASKS

□ - In Process
v - Close

DEPARTMENTAL OBJECTIVE:

KEY INDIVIDUAL TASKS	RESP'Y	QTR '91 1 2 3 4	QTR '92 1 2 3 4	QTR '93 1 2 3 4	LATER PERIOD
PLAN AND HOLD OPEN HOUSE HIGH SPEED/PRODUCTION MACHINERY	T. Root				
COMPLETE A-55 SLIDE PRESENTATION REVISION					
COMPLETE MMC SLIDE PRESENTATION REVISION					
COMPLETE TURNKEY ENGINEERING BROCHURE REVISION					
COMPLETE TURNKEY ENGINEERING SLIDES					
COMPLETE MONITORING SYSTEMS FLYER					
DEFINE OPEN HOUSE/SHOW RESPONSE BEGIN DIALOG ON IMTS 92 AND SET PLAN FOR P/M DEVELOP 1992 SEMINAR PLAN					
GENERATE APPLICATION PICTURES OF TURNKEYS FOR COLLATERAL MATERIAL					

97

SCHEDULE OF KEY INDIVIDUAL TASKS

□ - In Process
∇ - Close

DEPARTMENTAL OBJECTIVE:
PRODUCTION MACHINERY   PROMOTE IMAGE AS STATED □ IMAGE
PRODUCT PROMOTION   □ TURNKEY

KEY INDIVIDUAL TASKS	RESP'Y	QTR '91 1 2 3 4	QTR '92 1 2 3 4	QTR '93 1 2 3 4	LATER PERIOD
A-SS VIDEO PRODUCTION AND MAILING	T.Root Coordinator	✱∇			
APPLICATION EDGE / SATURN (CONTINUOUS)	"	✱∇		→	
TURNKEY MAILING TO 2000 CUSTOMERS	"	✱∇			
COMPLETE CORPORATE CATALOG AND MAILING TO KEY CUSTOMER CONTACTS	"	✱∇			
COMPLETE SECOND A-SS PRODUCTION (RELIABILITY/SYSTEM)	"	✱∇			
COMPLETE TECHNICAL ARTICLES ON SATURN PUBLISH	"	✱			
COMPLETE ARTICLE ON SWITZER PUBLISH		✱			

98

MIGRATION TO FLEX EQUIPMENT:

A REVIEW OF CRITICAL ASSUMPTION #2

by

Donald L. Jones
LeBlond Makino Machine Tool Company

August 28, 1991

MIGRATION TO FLEX EQUIPMENT - Critical Assumption #2

2

II. CONCLUSIONS

A. There will be a continued migration to flexible cells and systems because:

1. the cost to add flexibility to machining cells will continue to decline and

2. US manufacturing engineers are convinced flexibility is required for global competitiveness.

Other factors will play secondary roles in encouraging migration to flexible cells.

B. Passenger car and light truck part suppliers will NOT move to flexible cells in large numbers because:

1. part volume and contract length will limit the need for flexibility and

2. industry over capacity will squeeze profit margins and new equipment budgets, limiting funds to the minimum level possible.

The ratio of flexible cells to dedicated cells in this market heavily favors dedicated cells. We have seen and documented many purchases of flexible equipment by this industry, however the purchase of dedicated equipment will continue to dominate.

C. Medium and heavy truck part suppliers will continue to lead the way to flexible cells because:

1. part volume and customer demands will highlight the need for flexibility and

2. the fewer part suppliers per component type will be better able to maintain their margins.

D. Automotive suppliers will not pay a premium for flexibility because:

1. the money will not be available,

2. the need for flexibility will not be great nor will it be recognized by the financial review process and

3

3. competition among machine builders will limit premium pricing strategies.

E. Many of the advantages touted for horizontal machining centers with pallet handling are really advantages of parallel manufacturing when compared with serial manufacturing.

4

III. US SHIPMENTS

The U.S. Department of Commerce, Bureau of the Census, publishes statistics in their Current Industrial Reports series. Metalworking Machinery is covered by the MQ35W series of CIR. The report provides information on US shipments, imports, exports and apparent US consumption. LeBlond Makino Product Promotion subscribes to this report.

A.   US SHIPMENTS

US shipments of all metal working equipment, by dollar volume, unadjusted dollars, rose sharply from 1971 until the crash of 1981 to 1983.   1989 was the first year US shipments saw significant recovery.

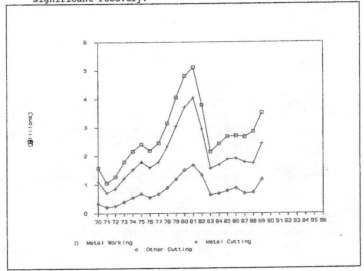

Other metal cutting equipment, the bottom line in Figure 1, consists of: machining centers, station type machines,

5

MIGRATION TO FLEX EQUIPMENT - Critical Assumption #2

broaching, sawing, tapping, EDM, ECM, and miscellaneous
cutting tools.

The following graph shows the fraction of metal cutting
equipment made up by the other metal cutting equipment
category.

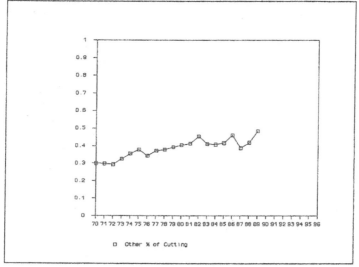

The share of other metal cutting equipment compared to metal
cutting equipment has slowly increased from 1970 to 1989 at
the expense of boring, drilling and milling machines.

6

MIGRATION TO FLEX EQUIPMENT - Critical Assumption #2

The Department of Commerce began reporting shipments of the
machining center and station type equipment portions of the
other metal cutting equipment shipments in 1982.

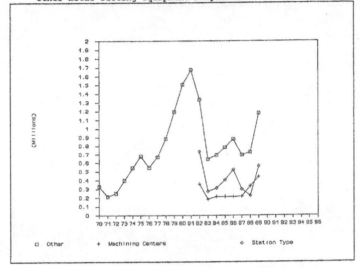

The key here is to identify the next category to grow large
enough to warrant redefinition of the reporting scheme.

The next category may be the flexible station type machine or
hybrid station type machine.

MIGRATION TO FLEX EQUIPMENT - Critical Assumption #2

The following graph shows what fraction of the other metal
cutting category is machining centers and what fraction is
station type machines.

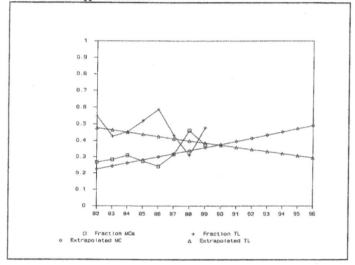

The straight lines show the least squares fit of the data and
extrapolation of the trend through 1996. There appears to be
a trend for an increase in the US shipments market share of
machining centers and a decrease in the market share of
station type machines.

8

IV. IMPORT PENETRATION

The pie chart to the right compares 1989 US shipments of machining centers to US consumption of machining centers.

Import penetration of this market is high.

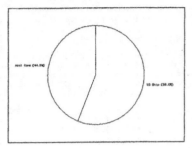

The pie chart to the right compares 1989 US shipments of station type machines to US consumption.

Import penetration of this market is low.

This reflects the intensive engineering effort required to supply a station type machine.

Perhaps LeBlond Makino can supply the engineering expertise and high quality product required by the station type users.

9

V.   SHARE PROJECTION

FORECASTS

The Market Intelligence Research Co., Mountain View, CA issued
market share projections. They see continued decline of the
milling machine share and the largest increase in the grinding
share (see "Modernizing Metalcutting", Manufacturing
Engineering, April 1990, article enclosed.)

The following graph shows the market share of machining
centers (the upper line) declining slightly after 1990 and the
station type share remaining flat.

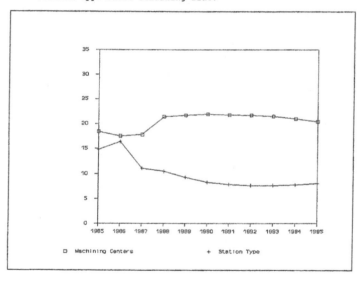

They predict that:

10

MIGRATION TO FLEX EQUIPMENT - Critical Assumption #2

"...builders trying to meet quality and productivity
goals will have more choices. Hybrid machines that
perform several functions will appear on the market.
When combined with transfer machines, these hybrids could
form a semidedicated automated package and shrink the
size of manufacturing cells."

Hybrid machines are being purchased and more "standard"
hybrids are available on the market.

11

VI. DEFINE ASSUMPTION TO VERIFY

     The purpose of this section is to clarify the meaning of
     critical assumption #2.

     CRITICAL ASSUMPTION #2

     "There will be a migration from transfer lines to flexible
     cells and systems."

     DEFINITIONS

     Migration -   Migration means the market share of flexible
                       cells and systems will increase faster than
                       the market share of transfer lines over the
                       next five years.

     Market Share -   Is the percentage of metal cutting equipment
                       consumption, by dollars, in North and South
                       America. However, for this report only the US
                       market is considered.

     Transfer line -   "A manufacturing system in which
                       individual stations are used for
                       dedicated purposes." Source Allen-
                       Bradley, A Glossary of CIM Terms,
                       CASA/SME, 1984, p.92. Rotary dial index
                       machines are a special type of transfer
                       line.

     Flexible Cells - A physical grouping of equipment that can
                       produce different parts with minimal
                       change over compared to the processing
                       time of the smallest desired batch.

     Flexible Systems - A physically connected group of equipment
                       to produce a variety of parts.

COMMENTS

1.   Flexible cells and systems can be many other things than HMCs
     with pallet handling.

2.   While transfer lines are based on serial manufacturing,
     flexible systems may be based on either serial or parallel
     manufacturing. The balance of advantages and disadvantages of
     parallel machining over serial processing may be a key area
     for determining which manufacturing environments will purchase
     flexible systems.

12

MIGRATION TO FLEX EQUIPMENT - Critical Assumption #2

3. If critical assumptions: #6, material substitutes and #7,
    market size, prove to be false, that is, we believe the
    overall metal cutting market will decrease in size, then the
    relative market share of transfer lines and flexible cells and
    systems becomes a secondary factor in strategic planning.

4. US companies evaluate investments in flexible systems
    differently than companies in other countries with vastly
    different wage rates, skill levels, energy costs, inflation
    rates, land costs and tax structures. Only the US market is
    considered in this report.

VII. SECONDARY ASSUMPTIONS

IMPLIED ASSUMPTIONS	COMMENTS
Flexibility is required to meet product life cycle demands.	Vehicle development lead time is expected to drop to 24 months by the year 2000 (Anderson Consulting, 6th Delphi Report, _Putting the Pieces Together_, p.72) but there is also a move towards modular vehicle subsystems (AC, p. 51.) which would decrease part proliferation.
	Life cycle demands in construction equipment, pumps and valves and other industries should be reviewed.
CNC adopts/allows design changes and this is a benefit to transfer line users.	Fixture changes can be expensive for a high volume system. Expertise for reprogramming may be a hurdle to change, for transfer line users.
Transfer lines equal inflexibility.	This is true by definition BUT, the hybrid machine has been purchased by many users (interview notes).
Transfer lines and dial indexes are not flexible	
Because of control costs.	
The cost of controls will	This is very unlikely. "...RISC will give machines in the

13

not decline rapidly.

$5,000 to $10,000 price range the processing power of 80486 based CISC machines now costing about $20,000." according to Standard & Poor's Industry Survey, Computers & Office Equipment, Basic Analysis, June 28, 1990, p.C79, this decline will be seen in CNC controls as well. CNC controls are based on the same chips. GEF sees continued price declines.

Because of axis motions.

The technology to provide three axes motion is not widely available.

Three axes units are available, see competitive products, such as from CELL CON.

However they do not have the spindle technology we have.

Transfer lines are primarily used in automotive machining.

This seems to be true based on interviews. However, dial transfers are also used in hydraulic valve machining and other industries.

Car model lives are shortening, reducing the production life of parts.

Vehicle sub systems counter this trend.

CNC machine life exceeds product life.

The MC86 may be built to last for five to ten years and meet this criteria, but is the A55?

CNC machine life is comparable or longer than transfer line life.

Transfer line stations are simpler. Transfer line stations use full bearing ways.

Part volumes are being reduced by car model proliferation.

The minimum economical assembly volume is estimated to be 100,000 by the year 2000 (AC, p.19). In July, 1991, Toyota said it will begin building a

14

$355 million car plant in Australia to build 100,000 cars per year. This sets a minimum per part volume of 100,000 pieces per year assuming only one piece per vehicle unlike calipers, control arms, and knuckles.

Frequent line change overs (weekly) required flexibility.	Automakers do not need change overs on a weekly basis. Change overs once a year maximum.
There is a trend to JIT.	The trend to JIT will be hampered in the US auto industry by: unpredictable customer buying, poor car assembler scheduling and focusing on bigger issues including continuous improvement and employee discipline.
CNC supports JIT better than transfer lines.	Depending on costly fixturing and program flexibility.
CNC reduces lead times.	Depending on demand order mix vs. system capacity.
CNC cuts job set up time.	If pallet, program and tool handling is provided.
The cost to add flexibility to a transfer line will remain constant.	This seems unlikely. Control costs will decrease.
The cost of CNC equipment relative to dedicated transfer lines will remain constant.	
Horizontal machining centers are flexible.	Depending on fixture, program and tools.
Transfer lines are supplied tooled.	Based on interviews, this is true.

15

113

MIGRATION TO FLEX EQUIPMENT - Critical Assumption #2

Transfer line users will buy horizontal machining centers with turnkeys and systems.

Based on sold projects this is true.

CNC is slower than transfer lines.

It may be that parallel manufacturing is slower, not CNC.

CNC provides better up time.

It may be that parallel manufacturing provides better up time. Or that better transfer line design could provide high up time.

Transfer lines must be serial manufacturing systems.

Small transfer lines could provide a fraction of the total volume required and provide some of the benefits of parallel manufacturing.

Transfer line users can/will adopt/adapt to CNC technology.

See inhibiting factors.

CNC technology can adapt to transfer line users.

?

Unattended machining is a benefit to transfer line users.

Not if unions stand in the way.

CNC improve spindle utilization.

?

CNC reduces per part costs.

?

The pace of migration to flex is dependant on the cost premium required for implementation.

True.

LeBlond Makino has a strategic advantage in meeting the needs of the target market.

16

114

VIII. FACTORS EFFECTING MIGRATION

This section summarizes the reasons for and against migration to flexible cell and system. Evaluating the importance of each factor and the balance between encouraging and discouraging forces may help determine the pace of migration to flexible cells.

A. Encouraging Migration To Flexible Cells and Systems

Computer Power/$

Desire To Be Perceived As A "State of the Art, High Tech" Manufacturer

Delivery Requirements

Simplify Production Control

JIT/Synchronous Manufacturing

    Set Up Time Reduction

    Reduce Costs Errors

Push To Increase Inventory Turns

"Journal Wisdom"

Compression of Product Life Cycles

Proliferation of Product Differentiation

Group Technology

Machine Part Complete

Prototype Needs

Access Wider Market

Reuse Equipment

Purchase Capacity In Increments

Reduce Project Risks

17

B.   Inhibiting Migration To Flexible Cells and Systems

Initial Costs

    Machine Costs

    Fixture Costs

    Tool Costs

    Runoff Costs

    Material Handling Costs

    System Costs

Transfer Line Mentality

    Cost Accounting Methods

        User

        Automotive Customers Of Our Users

        Utilization Assumptions

        No Production For Lunch, Breaks or Third Shift

        Changes Charged To Auto Assembler

    Manufacturing Engineering Methods

Multiple Process Streams

Unions

    GM's Job Guarantee Contracts

    No Unattended Machining

Special Operations

    Honing

    Bushing Pushing

    Line Boring

Operator Skills

18

MIGRATION TO FLEX EQUIPMENT - Critical Assumption #2

Direct Labor Costs

Maintenance Skills

Systems Management Costs

Environmental Requirements

Floor Space Costs

Failure To Recognize Volume Uncertainty Risks

Failure To Anticipate Product Change Requirements

Failure To Recognize the Quality Costs of Transfer Lines

Failure To Manage All Project Risks

19

117

Commentary by Mr. Donald Bowers, Former CEO

Dr. Sid Barton asked me to comment on my experiences in using his principles for strategic management, and I am glad to do this. Sid has been a lifelong student and practitioner of strategy, and these principles are an effective set of guidelines for any practitioner of strategic management. My comments are not about the situations, challenges, and opportunities that the companies faced where I applied his principles. Nor are the comments about the various personalities that participated in crafting and implementing the strategies. Rather, these comments are my perspectives on the strategy processes and tools that served me well for twenty years while leading three manufacturing companies and engaging a wide variety of managers and executives in developing and implementing strategy.

Strategy is all about setting and executing the agenda for a company. The chief executive officer's preeminent responsibilities are to be sure that a company is doing the right thing and doing it well. Given that strategy is the plan to achieve a desired future state, it is imperative that the CEO lead the development and implementation of his company's strategic plan.

Sid's strategic management tools and processes enable effective communication among the executive team in a dialogue that defines the company's agenda; sells its urgency; integrates its elements into the personal priorities of the team members; establishes closed-loop measurements for monitoring strategic success; and tests the plan constantly in an effort to uncover its vulnerabilities. I have discovered two lessons the hard way: (1) both strategy development and its implementation are better when multiple people with diverse perspectives are empowered to participate; and (2) a consistent and comprehensive understanding of anything worthwhile, and especially of strategy, requires a shared experience of discovery. Sid's principles for strategic management provide the CEO with the process for leading his team through this shared experience of discovery.

The following comments on the most important of Sid's processes and tools are provided to give you greater insight into my experiences:

1. **Vision:** As was seen in the 1992 U.S. presidential campaign, "that vision thing" can be troublesome for a leader, and this is especially true for the leader of a commercial business where the fundamental business model fails to generate increases in shareholder value. Sid describes vision as "a desired future state," and I have found it useful to think of a company's vision as being analogous to a high mountain peak on the horizon that serves as a constant reference to the traveler who must select from among many twisted roads on a long journey. This analogy may be overdone, but the vision needs to be beyond your reach in the near term in order to provide the organization with a sustained focus and orientation for choosing among competing strategies. If a company's vision is the articulation of its desired future state, then its strategy is the roadmap to arrive at this future state. The rest of the strategic planning tools are aids for developing the most robust of strategies to optimize success.

2. **Situation Analysis:** Strategy development is an iterative process that seeks to define a shared understanding of the best strategies that will mitigate the risks and secure the greatest gain in pursuit of the vision. The process is performed with limited facts and knowledge, what Sid refers to as "bounded rationality." This bounded rationality will present uncertainties that result in differences of opinion and spirited debate among the team members.

Sid does not describe the situation analysis in this book, but he introduced it as a valuable tool for initially engaging everyone in a discussion of environmental factors and sustaining the discussion by channeling what might otherwise have become discordant argument into a cataloging of certain and uncertain environmental factors. The teams invariably agreed that some environmental factors would have a certain and significant influence on the success of a strategy, and these were cataloged in the situation analysis. The teams also disagreed as to whether other environmental factors would have a certain and significant influence on strategic success, and these were cataloged in the critical assumptions (see below). Between the two lists, those critical environmental factors that were considered when developing, testing, and implementing strategy were cataloged for reference. It should be understood that the situation analysis and critical assumptions do not eliminate conflicting opinions; rather, they constructively channel the conflict to produce a stronger strategy.

3. **Strategic Statement:** The strategic statement includes five critical concepts that together provide a framework for more rigorously developing strategy.

    a.   **Strategic Goals**: As vision is a future state that is not achievable in the near term, the strategic goals should be stretch goals that are not achievable in the near term. There will always be some who resist goals that are not readily achievable; but it is important to explain that while tactical goals may be achieved within months, strategic goals generally require years to achieve. I have followed the familiar admonition "to beware of what you measure because you may get it" and set goals that will secure a worthy strategic improvement in pursuit of our vision. When writing strategic goals, I have found it useful to utilize SMART goals. *SMART* goals are *S*pecific, *M*easurable, *A*ction-oriented, *R*elevant, and *T*imely. SMART goals have helped the teams to draft better strategies.

b. **Growth Direction:** Sid has described the simple two-by-two matrix of new or current products/ services against new or current customers/markets as the key to this section, and while this definition is essential, I have found it useful to describe more precisely the characteristics of the target customers/ markets as well. Every group with whom I've worked has struggled over the conflict of new target market goals that do not incorporate all existing customers. However, when the vision is a "desired future state," we often conclude that our past failure to achieve higher sales and profits is the result of our having been looking in all the wrong places. In arguing against the exclusion of existing customers from the target for new business development, sales personnel will calculate the historical sales from the newly defined target markets and rhetorically ask if we can survive on that sales volume, or they will plead the case for loyalty to existing customers in rejecting the more restrictive strategic market target. The groups typically overcame this conflict by considering growth direction as the more highly focused definition of where the company would seek new business growth in pursuit of its vision and strategic goals while acknowledging a tactical commitment *to support* all existing customers. The more restrictive market targets led to more refined market analyses with greater confidence that the target markets were sufficiently large to support our objectives. And the more precise market targets led to more competitively differentiated strategies that were more certain of success.

c. **Competitive Advantage:** Most groups, when first asked to describe their company's competitive advantages, will recite a mantra of competitive advantages that may or may not be true and that may or may not have relevance to the business of today or the future. It is imperative that the team critically analyze their strategy and compile a list of competencies that are both *necessary* and *sufficient* to sustain competitive advantage, including (1) those competencies that the company truly possesses that are necessary for strategic success and deserving of investment to sustain; and (2) those competencies that are currently absent or currently insufficient but are necessary for strategic success and deserving of investment to develop and to sustain. This list will drive investment of money and human resources, so it must be highly focused and restricted to what is both necessary and sufficient for sustained competitive advantage.

d. **Driving Force:** Sid has referenced research by Tregoe and Zimmerman that identifies eight legitimate driving force factors that impact and influence the nature and direction (i.e., strategy) of any organization. It is worth repeating that Tregoe and Zimmerman's study of seventy-five firms concluded that each was fundamentally driven by one, and only one, of these factors. The driving force is not unlike "instinct" in an individual in that it strongly influences how a company approaches markets and reacts to competitive threats and new opportunities. And I have found benefit in driving analysis down to a more precise description of driving force. For example, it may be significant to know that a driving force of "products offered" may more precisely be a driving force of "hammers offered" as opposed to "forged tools offered." Driving force is a screen to sort out incompatibilities in strategy as Sid discusses in his book. I've also found driving force to be a useful concept for evaluating traditional and nontraditional competitors. We often discovered new insights when evaluating a competitor's behaviors against its presumed driving force and even more insight when predicting how a competitor would likely react to our strategic initiatives.

e.   **Generic Strategy:** Sid has referenced Michael Porter's five forces model for assessing the profit potential of industries and his generic competitive strategy matrix. Porter's five forces model provides great insight into strategy and is an excellent survey of competitiveness considerations. And the apparently simple distinction between "low cost" and "differentiated" generic strategies has provoked valuable discussions that reconciled perceived conflicts between low-cost solutions and low-cost machines.

f.   **Critical Assumptions:** As discussed above in the situation analysis section, I have found it quite valuable to catalog where there is agreement versus lack of agreement among team members in regards to our business environment. The teams initially agreed to disagree over items that were cataloged as critical assumptions, but it didn't stop there. This technique permitted the teams to proceed provisionally when drafting the initial strategy, but the lists of critical assumptions represented a backlog of future research work. The teams subsequently returned to the list and looked at sensitivity analyses to determine relative priority and to make individual or team assignments to complete desk research, market research, or other analyses that tested hypotheses and reduced or eliminated the uncertainty. In those cases where the uncertainty was eliminated, the strategy was reassessed in the freshly confirmed reality and modified as appropriate to mitigate the risk or to exploit the opportunity. And in those cases where uncertainty could not be eliminated but the risk to success was still high, the strategies were modified to mitigate the risk with the buy-in of the skeptics.

g. **Competitor Analyses:** The greatest portion of competitor analyses have admittedly been static analyses that were incorporated in the situation analysis; but the far more valuable competitor analyses were dynamic predictions of key competitors' reactions to the company's strategic initiatives. As with critical assumptions, dynamic competitor analyses were the result of continuing assignments to test and strengthen the strategy. There is significant gain in crafting refined strategies in a set competitive environment, but there is much greater gain in thinking through competitor's responses to perceived threats and crafting strategies for sustained success in a dynamic competitive environment. This work is analogous to a chess game in which checkmate is achieved by the player who successfully analyzes and predicts his opponent's every move.

h. **Key Strategies:** These strategy statements are frequently seen as the end result of strategic planning, but they more accurately represent the instant image of a dynamically evolving strategy. In my experience, the form of the written strategies has varied widely based upon the sense of the team as to how they should be expressed. My personal favorite was a strategic plan that described how we were achieving a new future state in five succinct statements. Good strategy is often so straightforward and disarmingly simple that people will initially shun it as being too obvious, too simple, and too inconsequential. They will think that the path to success must be more complicated than this! The first strategy that Sid facilitated with me was exactly this experience. What was adopted was not a new technology or a new business; rather it was a plan to replicate the experience of a few successful orders on a greatly expanded scale and to enhance the processes by which we executed those orders. The team had identified the target within the first two hours of analysis; but it was weeks later before we were convinced that this was the appropriate new strategy. That strategy ultimately drove a tenfold increase in targeted revenue and produced more than 50 percent of the sales of a much larger company.

i. **Linkage to Tactical Planning:** Strategic planning success is ultimately dependent on how well the employees of the company change the way they work. Few people have the ability to see the business simultaneously in the context of the present state and the future state. Most of us are set in our ways and comfortable with, if not consumed by, the daily rhythm of business, so we can not underestimate the importance of translating strategy into the context of the daily work of people in the company. In the LeBlond Makino example that Sid has included in this text the key individual tasks (KITS) were overkill and transitional, but they were seen by the team as necessary at the time to connect all employees to the strategy. New strategy requires significant effort to develop new processes and new tools to execute that strategy. Integrating the new strategy into an evolving pattern of the way employees work cannot be ignored, and I recommend a level of detail that is judged to be both necessary and sufficient by the employees who must execute the change.

j. Regularly Recurring Meetings to Enhance the Strategy: Strategy is iterative; it is dynamic; it is subject to "bounded rationality"; it is outside the present state; it is leadership; and it demands an allocation of appropriate effort on a recurring basis. At critical times of change, I've scheduled meetings on a weekly basis. At a minimum, I've found the strategic plan should be addressed formally at least twice per year.

Sid acknowledges in this book that managers will modify his basic strategy processes and tools, and I have done this repeatedly over the past twenty years based upon the circumstances faced, the needs of the team, and my evolving experience. Sid is a passionate and engaged professional who has studied strategic management for the past forty years. I share his passion for the activity, but I am not the student that he is. I have "gone to school" on his research and have found his model to be a malleable process that is readily shaped to incorporate new concepts and ideas. This durability is testament to the value of Sid's work. Thanks, Sid.

Example 2: Clermont Chamber of Commerce

Background

The Clermont Chamber of Commerce is located in Clermont County, Ohio. Clermont County is adjacent to Hamilton County, the location of the city of Cincinnati, Ohio. As such the chamber is one of several smaller county-based ones found in the counties that surround the city of Cincinnati.

Taking directly from the organization's Web site (www. clermontchamber.com), the following provides a brief description of the county itself as well as the Clermont chamber.

About Clermont County, Ohio

Whether you prefer the natural beauty of wide-open spaces or the cultural advantages of a major metropolitan area, you will be at home in Clermont County. The county, which celebrated its bicentennial in 2000, consists of friendly neighborhoods, villages, and towns that are nestled between urban and rural landscapes.

Located in southwestern Ohio, a few miles east of Cincinnati, Clermont County boasts a total land area of 459 square miles, or 293,760 acres. Batavia, the county seat but not the largest town, is centrally located in the county. Clermont's western border touches Anderson Township, Terrace Park, and Indian Hill, Ohio's wealthiest community. The eastern border is fronted by Brown County, where farms and woodlands flourish. To the north is Warren County, and to the south are the scenic Ohio River and the state of Kentucky.

Clermont consists of fourteen municipalities and fourteen townships, including such large communities as Amelia, Batavia, Bethel, Loveland, Milford, New Richmond, and Williamsburg. In many respects, Clermont views its largest town as the city of Cincinnati itself. This metropolis, located only a few miles west of the county across Anderson Township, offers virtually endless cultural and entertainment resources.

History of the Clermont Chamber

In 2009, the chamber celebrates forty successful years of service to the business community of Clermont County. Originally formed as a loose-knit coalition of business leaders set on attracting the University of Cincinnati to locate a branch in Clermont, we were officially chartered as a chamber of commerce in late 1969. Over the years, we have grown to play a major leadership role in the economic development of Clermont and its surrounding communities. In 2002, the Clermont chamber was awarded Chamber of the Year at the National Association of Membership Development (NAMD).

What Is the Clermont Chamber?

The Clermont chamber is a voluntary association of businesses, professionals, and individuals working together to enhance the Clermont community.

What Is the Goal of the Clermont Chamber?

The goal of the Clermont chamber is to make Clermont an enviable place to live and work.

Who Leads the Clermont Chamber?

The approximate one thousand businesses, professionals, and individuals comprising its membership lead the Clermont chamber. A sixteen-member board of directors governs the Clermont chamber. The president/CEO, with the support of a staff of eight professionals, manages the day-to-day operation of the chamber.

Motivation for Strategic Management

In the mid-1990s, the chamber found itself in a transitional state. As described in the history section above, the chamber had been started in 1969 with the primary goal of attracting businesses to locate to Clermont County. The chief architect and driver of the chamber throughout this entire developmental period was a man named Ed Parish. Mr. Parish, as president of the organization, was a "larger than life" kind of person who set the agenda of the chamber according to his personal view of what needed to be done. Mr. Parish was particularly focused on economic development of the county and had been personally responsible for wooing a number of businesses to locate to Clermont County. However, as the chamber evolved and grew and the county they served was doing the same, the board of directors realized that when Mr. Parish left, the organization needed to define exactly what the role of the chamber needed to be going forward. They also felt a need (and an opportunity) to establish a more inclusive, consensus-based governance process.

In addition, as Mr. Parish was transitioning out, the current executive vice president of the organization (Mr. Denny Begue, heir apparent to the staff leadership position) desired guidance as to where the chamber needed to go in the future. Unlike the previous example in which the president of the for-profit organization was empowered to make final decisions on direction, the chamber was governed by a board of directors made up of volunteers selected from the membership. Compounding this situation was the fact that each year a new volunteer board member became chair of the board. This often resulted in a totally new agenda for staff along with different priorities. Therefore, the full-time chamber staff was frustrated because they could not establish any momentum for programs or initiatives when they were changed annually.

As it turned out, one of the board members of the chamber was a vice president of the Makino Corporation. He recommended that the chamber engage me to assist in the development of a strategic management system to address the needs of the chamber. It was this context in which the process was begun.

Group Selected to Develop the Strategic Management System

The exact makeup of the initial planning group is described in detail in the executive summary of the example document that follows. However, to summarize here, the group was established by the board of directors and consisted of fourteen persons representing key constituencies of the chamber. The goal was to have a transparent process that was representative of those most affected by the chamber. An especially important participant was the senior administrator of the county government. This was important, because the economic development role in the county actually was the responsibility of the county government and not a group that essentially represented the business interests of its members.

Thus the challenge for this group was far different than that described in the first example, in that the decision rule was consensus and not chief executive fiat. Obtaining the consensus of the group required considerable time, energy, and commitment by all participants. The fact that to develop the initial strategic document required eight half-day meetings over four months is a testament to the commitment of this largely volunteer group. However, they all seemed to appreciate that this task was critical to laying a foundation for the future of the chamber.

The Process

The process used by the chamber is fully laid out in the following example document in the words of the planning group. However, what is not described is that each year, a new planning committee met to review and update as desired the strategic statement and its critical assumptions. A full board of director's meeting was then charged with approving the plan. Based on this approved plan, the staff prepared detailed yearly plans and actions based on the functional strategies laid out in the document.

The most important use of the written strategic statement document, however, may have been that it allowed the president of the organization to maintain a more consistent direction from year to year. This is no small challenge when operating an organization that depends on the assistance and goodwill of volunteer members. I will leave this point to be addressed in the commentary section by Mr. Begue as he reviews his perspective on the impact of this process on the success of the chamber. My own hope is that in at least some small measure, that implementation of this process resulted in the Clermont chamber receiving Chamber of the Year of the United States in 2002. However, I will defer to Mr. Begue for that assertion.

Example of Output

What follows is the completed document developed by the planning committee and presented to the full board of directors for approval in the fall of 1996. I have included the full document because it describes the process as well as the specific details of the plan.

♦ ♦ ♦

Strategic

Planning

Process

Clermont Chamber of Commerce
Strategic Planning Process

Executive Summary

Objectives

Process

Definitions

Strategic Statement

Critical Assumptions

Principal Activities

- Goal Statements
- Target Market
- Competitive Advantage
- Growth Direction
- Driving Force
- Generic Competitive Strategy

Development of Functional Strategies

Action/Work Plans

Implementation of Strategic Management System

Executive Summary

The Strategic Planning Committee ("SPC") is pleased to present its recommendations to the Board of Directors of the Clermont Chamber of Commerce.

The SPC was conceived by the Executive Committee and endorsed by the Board of Directors to develop a strategic planning and thinking process to assure the Clermont Chamber of Commerce would continue as a progressive and highly effective organization, supporting, promoting and assuring a strong business climate in Clermont County. Its work consumed a period of more than four months including eight sessions led by our facilitator, Sidney L. Barton, Ph.D., Head of the Department of Management, College of Business Administration, University of Cincinnati. A consultant to profit and non-profit organizations, Dr. Barton's specialty is strategic planning management.

The SPC included fourteen individuals, four from the Chamber's management, six from the current Board of the Chamber, a Clermont County senior administrator, a former executive of the Greater Cincinnati Chamber of Commerce and two former chairs of our Chamber. The members were Dean Roger Barry, Dennis W. Begue, Joseph Boruszewski, James D. Buckner, Daniel L. Earley, Jeanne Feldkamp, Richard T. Findlay, Paul Flood, Gregg J. MacMillan, James L. Meyer, Edward J. Parish, Chris Smith, Matthew Van Sant and A. Steve Wharton.

The development of a strategic planning process becomes the **foundation for decision making** and **policy formation** along with **improved internal communication, learning** and **attention to strategic issues.** We believe this process is critical to our viability as the environment in which we operate is changing rapidly and we need to adapt to external influences continuously.

1

134

The process involves designing a framework for decision making which is unique to the circumstances of the Clermont Chamber. Specifically, the SPC chose to develop an overall **Corporate Goal** for the Chamber which became the fundamental overarching purpose for all Chamber activities. We then identified two very different "**businesses**" or types of activities which, taken together, were critical to the achievement of our corporate goal. These "businesses" are **Economic Development** and **Membership Services**. In the process of our discussions, it became clear that while these businesses have very different **goals, target markets, competitive advantages, growth directions, driving forces** and **generic competitive strategies** (i.e. key elements of a strategic decision making framework), they are synergistic and essential for the attainment of the overall goal.

Once these elements were identified, **critical assumptions** which underlay our strategies were developed and established as a basis for future assessment and monitoring. In addition, to support the attainment of the business strategies developed, functional strategies necessary to support them were brainstormed. These functional strategies will form the basis for staff development of the annual action/work plans.

It is important to note that this work represents our best shot at providing direction for the Chamber, but it is only the beginning. We have found that in the short time we have met to develop this plan, our mutual understanding of the issues and of each other's viewpoints has grown tremendously. We, therefore, urge continual challenge and enhancement of the ideas presented herein. We must remember that this strategic framework must assist our staff and volunteers in deciding how they spend their time and money. If it does not do that, or we do not choose to use it, we will have wasted our time in its development.

We believe firmly that the ongoing leadership of strategic planning must rest with the **top executive** and the **top lay leadership** to continue our focus on **what we should be doing** to meet our strategic objectives.

2

STRATEGIC PLANNING

Objectives

We developed this process as a foundation for:

- Decision making and policy formation

- Continual attention to strategic issues

- Management communication

- Organizational learning and continual improvement

- Efficient environmental screening (awareness of one's environment)

- Development of integrated and supported functional plans

. . . . all in an environment of rapid and often unpredictable change.

A Process:

Strategic planning is a continual process that allows for the "screening" of ideas, concepts and possible actions for decision making. The process is part of the organization's culture as a "strategic management system" - a way of thinking strategically to permit the organization to adjust its plans as situations change. It affords the ability to adapt to change and take advantage of opportunities.

3

STRATEGIC PLANNING

DEFINITIONS

Strategy: The pattern of decisions which reveals and reflects the goals of the organization and the means being employed to achieve the goals. *"What you do, not what you say you are doing."*

Corporate Goal: The ultimate purpose of the organization . In other words, the outcome which is desired as a result of the efforts of the organization.

Mission Statement: A framework which provides guidance and/or criteria for decisions (strategy) of the organization. This framework reflects the fundamental belief system of the organization (assumptions or "myths"). It states what the organization wants to achieve and how it intends to achieve it.

Strategic Management System

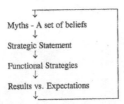

Myths - A set of beliefs

Strategic Statement

Functional Strategies

Results vs. Expectations

Myth: A model of reality; the beliefs/assumptions about:

· The industry
· The competitors
· The market/clients
· Yourself
· Others

which form the foundation of your actions and decisions (strategy).

"You need to accept that your beliefs may not be correct."

4

137

Strategic Statement: Elements include

- Strategic goals/vision
- Target markets
- Competitive advantages
- Growth directions
- Driving forces
- Generic competitive strategy (focused vs. broad)

Note: All elements should be interdependent and consistent with each other.

Functional Strategies: These address the question: "What should be done to support and/or facilitate the corporate or business level strategy?" "What objectives are necessary to help us put together an operational plan?"

Possible functional strategies include:

- Human resources
- Finance
- Technology
- Marketing
- Procurement/purchasing
- Lobbying

Goal Statement: A statement that truly drives the Chamber's actions. Why does the Chamber exist? If there are multiple goals, what is the order of importance? Are they compatible? How can they be measured? If they can't be measured, they probably have limited value as you cannot determine how your activities are affecting it.

Target Market: Are there different segments of the market? What are the characteristics of each? Is one segment more important relative to the Chamber's goals? Realize that a target market doesn't mean you are restricted only to serving that group, only that these people/organizations represent preferred clients which you will attempt to influence.

Competitive Advantages: What you do best that is the key to your success and can be used to gain advantage over competitors. The best such advantages are ones which are unique to you and/or difficult for competitors to copy. All activities you choose to do should take advantage of these characteristics or should serve to enhance one or more of them.

Growth Direction: How you intend to grow the organization. Options include, but are not limited to, new services to existing clients, new clients for old services, geographic growth, new services to new clients, etc. This direction should be consistent with the best use of your competitive advantages to achieve your goals.

5

138

Driving Force: The factor that determines what products and services are offered to which markets. There are several possibilities, such as market needs, products offered, capabilities, technology, etc. Once again, it must be linked to and consistent with the rest of the elements of the strategic statement.

Generic Competitive Strategy: This positions us against our competition:

Example: Hotel industry

	Niche	Broad Market
Low Cost	La Quinta	Motel 6
Differentiated By Value	Ritz Carlton	Marriott

6

STRATEGIC STATEMENT
Overall Chamber Corporate Goal

"Promote a vibrant, positive business climate to provide a high quality of life for those who live or work in Clermont County. "

Committee Discussion: *Considerable brainstorming, revising and refining of this statement occurred throughout the first half of our sessions. Possible strategic goals beyond those set forth above included sustaining the Chamber as a foundation for free enterprise and economic growth; the retention, creation and expansion of business investments; retention and expansion of political influence; assurance of the Chamber's financial strength; product offerings to enhance members' profitability; enhancement of job growth; increase tax base and property values; attraction of new businesses and expansion of existing businesses; provide for county information; foster growth of small businesses.*

However, after much discussion, these other alternatives seemed like a means to an end, rather than an end in themselves. Concensus of the SPC was that the above goal represented the ultimate "raison d'etre" (reason for being) of the Chamber.

7

140

CRITICAL ASSUMPTIONS

Criteria for critical assumptions: If the assumptions are not true, the strategy will have to change; we must have data to support our assumptions. If we are not certain of their validity, we must test the assumptions.

A. **Local business growth can be sustained**

Committee Discussion: We believe that we enjoy some level of insulation from the national and international economies, and, therefore, the county can be expected to sustain its local growth assuming no catastrophic recession/depression. This is implicit in our belief that a vibrant Clermont County business climate can be maintained regardless of outside business cycles. Periodic action may be necessary to assess this assumption proactively.

B. **Cooperation between the public and private sectors will continue**

Committee Discussion: We believe this is paramount to achieve our strategic goal. This assumption requires continuous monitoring and attention, as it is reflected in our lobbying functional strategies discussed in the next section.

C. **Enhance relationship with Greater Cincinnati Chamber**

Committee Discussion: We believe our economic development success (especially the recruitment of new businesses to Clermont County) is enhanced with a cooperative effort with G.C.C. Additionally, we believe we can strengthen our relationships with other chambers through various collaborative efforts. This assumption requires a proactive effort to strengthen and enhance this relationship.

D. **Businesses have an interest in the quality of life in the county**

Committee Discussion: We probably do not know how businesses (especially small companies) feel toward enhancing quality of life issues. This assumption needs to be assessed via survey and continual personal assessment to assure we are on the right track.

E. **The Chamber represents a good value to its members**

Committee Discussion: This is "basic" to our retention of our membership base. We need to better understand why members stay and why they drop out. This is essential to our future viability.

8

141

F.   "More" (members) is "better"

Committee Discussion: Reasons for more members include greater political clout, greater resources, more volunteers, improved "buying power", expanded networking and increased communication of business/economic issues to business community. Concerns include staff resources, costs to service.

Conclusions: "More" members is "better" provided dues cover marginal costs. Consider tiered membership package levels (by size, by type of business or by utilization of services). "Something for everybody, but not everything for everybody."

G.   Volunteer time will continue to be available to the Chamber

Committee Discussion: It is clear that volunteer efforts and participation are critical to the Chamber's activities. However, people are being asked to do more with less and the Chamber may find fewer people available. This requires continual monitoring as well as design of volunteer activities which are more efficient in use of time so as to maintain this invaluable resource.

9

142

CHAMBER ACTIVITIES

We identified two principal activities or businesses of the Chamber:

- **ECONOMIC DEVELOPMENT**
- **MEMBERSHIP SERVICES**

Committee Discussion: *We believe we have two basic activities that are necessary to achieve our corporate goal. Consensus of the Committee was that both of these activities were absolutely essential, yet fundamentally strategically different, such that two separate, yet synergistic, strategies are required to achieve our goal.*

We believe economic development is the overall "driver"; however, a strong and growing membership base with valuable membership services is critical to our achieving success in economic development (through clout and members' education and understanding of economic development's role/impact).

The economic development role of the Chamber historically has been unique for Chambers and that without this role, the Clermont Chamber can have limited impact on the corporate goal. As such, economic development must continue to be uppermost in our minds in all activities which are undertaken. In short, this "business" represents a core competence which cannot be "contracted out" or sacrificed if the Chamber is to remain a viable entity.

10

ECONOMIC DEVELOPMENT
Strategic Elements

<u>Goal Statement:</u> Maintain and enhance our <u>leadership role</u> in increasing jobs (creation and retention) and business and public investment in the county.

Committee Discussion: *Leadership role is underlined here because of the crucial importance this suggests. The SPC believes that in order to meet our corporate goal, we must maintain and enhance our leadership role for economic development in the County. We believe we are uniquely qualified and positioned (see competitive advantages listed below) to do this.*

<u>Target Market:</u> Existing businesses and new businesses with high quality jobs.

Committee Discussion: *Existing businesses provide the vast majority of job growth, not new businesses. Need to develop formalized program that focusses on retention and expansion. How do we define characteristics of businesses we wish to cultivate? We must be mindful of tax base from all business segments (e.g. retail). When opportunities exist to "leverage" resources (e.g. Meijer road improvement), we must seize the moment. We wish to evaluate the quality of jobs in all areas of the county (some jobs may be more attractive to some rural areas that may be unattractive elsewhere). While we will not place emphasis in some areas, this does not mean we will not respond to non target market type businesses for support, it means we will not be proactive in seeking them out and developing them. However, high quality jobs are consistent with the corporate goal of the Chamber.*

<u>Competitive Advantages:</u> Access to power, to Greater Cincinnati Chamber, to elected officials; significant ability to influence public officials; respect of business community; continuity of effort and one-stop economic development package.

Committee Discussion: *The SPC believes the Chamber is unique in the county in having these advantages, and further, that these advantages will not easily be obtained by any other group. We must focus on those activities which use and further enhance these advantages.*

<u>Growth Direction:</u> Encourage light manufacturing, R & D, corporate and divisional headquarters, service, warehouse and distribution and growth of existing businesses.

Committee Discussion: *Consistent with our target market and overall corporate goal, programs directed at taking our current economic development services to these type firms in a proactive way is key to success.*

<u>Driving Force:</u> Market needs of the business-to-business community and economic resilience through diversity.

Committee Discussion: *This means we must be cognizant of what our target market needs in the way of economic development, and not merely what we currently offer. While we believe our current offerings and the needs of our target market are consistent, any new services directly provided by the Chamber staff must be both needed by our target and consistent with activities which take advantage of our competitive advantages. Services not based on what we do best should be provided by others.*

<u>Generic Competitive Strategy</u> - Broad differentiation.

Committee Discussion: *The Chamber is renowned for personalized attention. No other place can a firm visit which can provide the broad personalized attention that the Chamber can. This must continue to be a characteristic of Chamber economic development services to achieve our goal of Leadership.*

11

144

MEMBERSHIP SERVICES
Strategic Elements

Goal Statement: Value of services must exceed price; cost effective/productivity-enhancing services to increase members' profitability; sufficient membership base to maintain political clout and increase membership market share.

Committee Discussion: *This multi-goal statement reflects several aspects of the role of membership services in achieving the corporate goal. It suggests services must be cost effective, assist with membership profitability and provide political clout to synergistically support the economic development activity.*

Target Market: Those businesses that are located in Clermont County.

Committee Discussion: *While we wish to include all interested businesses as members, our emphasis will be those domiciled in the county. This decision is based on a belief that ~~only~~ those firms which are located in the county should be of ~~concern~~ relative to our corporate goal.*

Competitive Advantages: Staff knowledge of the county and its resources; cost-effective dues and service structure; diverse and valuable product and service offerings.

Committee Discussion: *Once again, the SPC believes that the only services which the Chamber should offer directly are those which leverage and/or enhance these advantages. We should not attempt to be all things to all people. Explore opportunities to enhance our competitive advantage through collaboration efforts with other chambers.*

Growth direction: Expand penetration of products and services to existing members.

Committee Discussion: *If the premise is that the services offered by the Chamber are indeed profit enhancing for members, we should attempt to increase utilization of all these services, consistent with our overall corporate goal, and not focus on expansion of membership regardless of service utilization. We should pursue alliances internally and externally to achieve our corporate goal.*

Driving Force: Market needs of businesses in Clermont County for cost-effective and productivity-enhancing business services.

Committee Discussion: *All services, current and future, should be based on this factor, in conjunction with the competitive advantages listed above.*

Generic Competition Strategy: Broad based, cost-effective services

Committee Discussion: *Unlike economic development, which is personalized and differentiated, we should be focused on providing member firms the most cost effective productivity enhancing services available. When we cannot, we should refer members to the lowest cost source, consistent with our overall objectives. In brief, we should truly be looking out for member interest and not Chamber self-interest.*

12

145

ECONOMIC DEVELOPMENT
Functional Strategies
*"What we must do to implement our strategic goal to
support our E.D. activity"*

Human Resources: *SPC believes the following HR needs are essential to supporting the ED strategy: Need Senior level ED person, dedicated to this activity, understands business needs and role of ED, has good networking ability, proven leadership and communication skills. Importance of this function requires succession development plan be in place to assure continuity.*

Marketing Plan: *To assure leadership, need to widely publicize ED success and value of Chamber to this success, along with the role of the Chamber. We also need to be proactive, per our target market and growth direction, to establish more formal programs for ED to target firms within the county and without. In short, we need a focused marketing plan for our ED activity. We should promote ED "ripple effect". Also recommended is a staff member dedicated to the marketing/promotion function.*

Finance: *Need to assess financial requirements to support this activity. SPC suggests developing a funding campaign which is self-supporting (i.e. does not depend on funds from membership services). Suggestions include grants, joint ventures, fees for ED services (which currently are free), tiered pricing structure (where fees vary with extent of services required), fees to non-SBDC clients, etc. Desire is to be aggressive in selling ED services to key county firms.*

Lobbying: *Current focus of activities is township and county. SPC suggests a coordinated plan be developed to be issued specific across a broad range of governmental jurisdictions. Issues need to be carefully selected to be consistent with overall corporate goal, as well as the ED activity goal.*

Governance: *We need "balance" of talents, experience and representation at Board level. To increase influence, need to cultivate "influential" leaders of large firms in the county for Chamber Board. Board roles and procedures need to reflect efficient participation to effectively recruit local business leaders. Board should always reflect membership interests.*

13

146

MEMBERSHIP SERVICES
Functional Strategies
*"What must we do to implement our strategic goal and to support
our Membership Services activity"*

Market Research: Assess penetration of current services to current members, determine relative impact of products/services on members' profitability, and assess other products and services which could utilize the Chamber's competitive advantages.

Product Development: Develop and/or emphasize services that are cost effective and contribute to members' success. Assess who competition is and what they are doing. Attempt to develop packages of related services to facilitate increased penetration. Also, use the "community service" component of membership to bring value to other members and the community consistent with the overall corporate goal (e.g. use influence to have government officials present informational talks for members). Assess current and planned activities for "fit" with the strategic statement so as to select what you do and what you outsource/eliminate.

Promotion: Need to develop an awareness campaign for the Chamber and its services/products to the target market. Should have a theme which expresses "who we are", "why we are different", and "why that difference is valuable". Identify those markets that are likely segmented by size (i.e. needs vary) and promote differently to each. Stress the productivity enhancing nature of the services/products. Promotion should highlight the excitement and vitality of the organization as an agent for the target markets best interests (i.e. use the "Not-For-Profit" aspect of the Chamber to emphasize that whatever is best for the client is best for the Chamber!)

Selling: Assess profitability of products/services which fit other strategic criteria, and emphasize what makes the Chamber money (i.e. as long as product is most cost effective for membership, any marginal revenue can go toward lowering cost of membership). Develop a specific selling plan which reflects increased penetration of current accounts.

Pricing: Per strategic goal, wish to be cost-effective, yet need to be incrementally profitable. This may require a tiered pricing approach based on the "bundle" of service desired. Assess pricing of other similar organizations for ideas.

Human Resources: Senior level executive, dedicated to this activity, understands business needs of members and has proven creative, promotional and communication skills.

Finance: Need to assess financial resources to support this activity. Believe membership services should be self-supporting through dues, fee services and event activities.

14

ACTION/WORK PLANS

Prepared by staff to achieve functional strategies that address the two principal activities of economic development and membership services.

Board "approves" plans and then "monitors" performances vs. goals.

15

STRATEGIC MANAGEMENT SYSTEM

The success of strategic planning will continue if the board and management treat it as an on-going process - a way of thinking, of decision making. It will never be "complete," it will always require refinement and change to address the rapidly evolving climate in which we operate.

The key thing to remember is that to be useful, decisions about committing resources and which activities to pursue must be guided by the Strategic Statement. If they are not, then either change the Statement to make it useful as a framework for decision making or don't bother to do strategic planning at all. In any event, you will have a strategy, whether you consciously develop one or not.

16

149

Commentary by Mr. Denny Begue, Former President of the Clermont Chamber

The strategic planning process did not begin until after two years of discussion to determine if this was any value to the chamber. That was always the challenge with thirty volunteer directors—getting consensus particularly as it related to long-term planning.

Once the decision was made to move forward with a strategic planning process even though several were not sure that there was any benefit, the process was painful. The group of volunteers needed to be honest and straightforward rather than being politically correct. Dr. Barton was extremely patient with these business and community volunteers. We all learned to understand what he meant by "Can you live with it?" As difficult as it was for the first few meetings, important issues were put on the table for probably the first time ever for the chamber.

After finally learning the consensus building part of the planning process, all of us began to make great progress. Dr. Barton's outline for strategic planning helped the chamber to understand our "reason for being," and we were able to articulate our principal activities. This process was unique at the time for not-for-profits but helped keep us on our mission year after year even with annual volunteer leadership changes.

The chamber for its size was a national leader in our economic development and workforce development programs. We were consistently in the top tier of our national peer group in nearly every membership related category. Living our mission every day and continually defining our principal activities helped us achieve the distinction of the 2002 National Chamber of the Year for mid-sized chambers of commerce.

Dr. Barton started the Clermont chamber with a great process in 1996. To the best of my knowledge, strategic planning is still an annual process with the chamber staff and volunteer leadership. The continuous benefit to the chamber staff was to keep a sharp focus on activities that supported the mission and to appropriately allocate financial and human resources to accomplish our goals and objectives. Volunteer leaders now had a process to follow if they wanted to change the direction rather than just following the leader for that particular year.

Example 3: Rotex Inc.

Background

As their Web site (www.rotex.com) states, "From grist mills to precision screeners and computer-controlled analyzers—a century and a half of innovative response to customer needs. In 2004, as we celebrate our 160th year, ROTEX is now the oldest manufacturer of capital goods in the Cincinnati community.

FOR OVER ONE HUNDRED YEARS, ROTEX has been a pioneer and global leader in the development of screening equipment and technology for the process industries. ROTEX engineers and manufactures a full line of leading-edge screening equipment, feeders, conveyors, and automated analyzers serving a global market in such industries as chemical processing, food processing, mineral processing, plastic compounding, and agribusiness.

Our innovative product line includes:

» Gyratory and Vibratory Screeners and Sifters for Dry Applications

» Liquid-Solid Separators for Wet Applications

» Automated Particle Size Analyzers

» Vibratory Feeders and Conveyors

» Aftermarket Parts and Service"

As their history and longevity attest, Rotex has been a creative and innovative organization. They have had to be to survive and prosper for over 160 years. Their application of strategic planning to their business is no different. Over fifteen years before engaging me to facilitate their planning process, they had initiated a formal yearly strategic planning activity. For a company of their size, this was very forward looking and frankly unusual. Nonetheless, they applied basic strategic planning approaches to their business.

Around 2005, as a result of the retirement of their former facilitator as well as a desire to try a different approach to planning, they engaged me to assist them. The primary business of the firm is designing and manufacturing dynamic machinery to provide separation for all types of commodity applications. Secondarily, their other main business is providing spare parts for the machines they sell. Their markets are international in scope, but they cover the world from single manufacturing and sales headquarters in the United States and Europe. The world headquarters for Rotex is located in Cincinnati, Ohio. The primary sales of the firm are handled through independent sales representatives, with an occasional direct salesperson where it makes sense.

Group Selected to Develop the Strategic Management System

Mr. Bill Herkamp has been president and CEO since 2002. Bill selected a diverse and representative group from headquarters along with the top two executives from Rotex Europe to populate the strategy group. Headquarters personnel included the heads of the parts division, machine sales, research and development, and manufacturing, along with additional key managers from the sales and manufacturing departments. The chief financial officer participated and served the role of scribe for all meetings. Lastly, the former president and CEO, Bill Lower, was invited to participate as well when available to provide additional background and expertise.

The Process

Rotex employs a fairly disciplined process that begins in the spring. In April, Mr. Herkamp and a select, smaller group of senior managers meet with the outside facilitator to determine what the emphasis will be for that year's strategic planning process. For the initial year I worked with them (2005), I presented the process model described previously, and they agreed to use it to see how it would work for them. In subsequent years, different approaches were selected based on what the top management felt was most important to address at that time. These different approaches and the rationale for using them are briefly described in the material that follows. In effect, what the group did was to continually refine their understanding of their business and how they wanted to go about achieving their goals. This process allows for maximum innovation and creativity. It also keeps the process from becoming routinized to the point that it becomes boring and repetitive. Actually, this had become the case with the previous process, as every year an extensive SWOT analysis was prepared. Unfortunately, the value of the information had become less than helpful, as it tended to repeat the same things year after year. As a result, it was little more than a "make work" assignment that did not result in additional useful learning.

The second step in the process involves the full group meeting in June to discuss the approach to be used in that year. Specific assignments are made to all the participants to gather information and develop material to be used in the three-day, off-site planning meeting that occurs in the fall. This provides the executives time to do research and prepare documents for this fall meeting. The material developed in this fall meeting provides the basis for the operational plans that are developed between the fall meeting and the end of the calendar year.

Unlike the previous two examples, in which actual plan documents are included in the output section, only summary information is provided here. The reason is that this plan material represents fairly recent strategy deliberations that could provide information directly useful to competitors. However, the material presented is intended to show how the group modified their assignments each year in order to optimize the time used and best assist their resource allocation decisions.

Examples of Output

Detailed information about specific material developed in the first year (2005) applying the process model described above is not presented. However, what follows is the description of the process used in year two (2006), which refers in general terms to the strategic statement developed in 2005.

It should be noted that the primary achievement of the first-year planning process was discovery and recognition of a very specific target market of applications, the "sweet spot" for which their products and technology were particularly well suited. This helped them focus their attention on their most profitable niche and design marketing and sales strategies to take full advantage of this target.

The determination in the spring of 2006 was that this fundamental strategic statement and the corresponding critical assumptions developed in 2005 were still valid but that what was most important was to make sure that the infrastructure was in place to achieve the desired goals. Thus the actual description of the 2006 process is presented here.

ROTEX

STRATEGIC BUSINESS PLANNING PROCESS

2006

Introduction

The following process is based on the assumption that Rotex will continue with the basic strategic direction developed over the last few years. This allows Rotex to develop strategic initiatives consistent with the elements of this basic corporate strategy without revisiting the fundamental aspects of this foundational strategy.

Specifically, Rotex will continue to select products and markets based on their proprietary gyratory motion, which provides superior separation for a certain class of product separation characteristics (i.e., the application "sweet spot"). They will continue to emphasize marketing and sales of their products wherever this motion can provide competitive advantage. Further, they will stress the superior performance of their products as the primary selling point as opposed to low price.

It is recommended that the assumptions implicit in this strategy be periodically challenged if/when results associated with this strategy do not meet expectations.

Current Process

1. **Confirm corporate goal.** This step is important to provide a basis for assessment of the applicability

and priority of the various initiatives to be developed later.

2. **Develop strategic initiatives that support the goal**. Based on the collective knowledge and experience of the executive staff, a set of strategic initiatives felt to provide the best alternatives to achieve the corporate goal consistent with the corporate strategy are developed. These initiatives should outline, where alternate approaches exist, roughly how the initiative will be pursued (e.g., require local manufacturing, rep sales, etc.).

3. **For each strategic initiative quantify the current year and long-term opportunity**. In effect, this is the *opportunities/threats* assessment for each initiative. Based on best knowledge, preliminary market potential both for the immediate and long term (normally based on assumed market share and total market potential) is developed, along with any obvious threats associated with the opportunity. Key assumptions for this preliminary estimate should be listed for later referral.

4. **Develop a process description of the key business processes and flow chart**. In this step, each manager responsible for a key business process is asked to develop the major elements of the processes assigned to them.

5. **Use the flow chart of the key business processes to determine the strengths and weaknesses of each strategic initiative**. In this step, using the business process map developed in step 4, each manager will assess the *strengths and weaknesses* of their process in support of each strategic initiative. When all process S/Ws for each initiative are combined, an initial representation of the nature of each opportunity will be complete.

6. **Determine the critical assumptions for each strategic initiative**. In this step, the entire team will develop critical assumptions and questions related to each strategic initiative. For reference, a critical assumption is one that is both uncertain and, if not true, would influence your decisions concerning the attractiveness of that initiative. These assumptions should cover both the *opportunities/threats* and *strengths/weaknesses* developed above. Each of these assumptions/questions will be assigned to an individual to gather as much information as possible on this issue in preparation for the planning retreat in August. Also, a team leader will be assigned to coordinate all people working on assignments associated with a specific initiative for presentation of that initiative at the retreat.

7. **Identify specific actions that are needed to achieve the goals for each strategic initiative**. Between step 6 and the planning retreat, each person responsible for a process should determine a rough plan and cost necessary to adequately support attainment of the goal for each initiative by that process. When combined with all other cost estimates and estimates of sales and profit margin, a rough ROI for each initiative can be obtained. Probabilities assigned to these estimates will provide management with an idea of the confidence level of the information.

8. **August retreat.** At this retreat, each team leader assigned to an initiative will coordinate a presentation of all information available related to each initiative. This report should include information on the assigned assumptions and questions as well as the proposed plans and costs associated with attaining the goal sales and profits. The level of confidence associated with attainment of goals should be included. Based

on these presentations and deliberations by the executive planning team, priorities and assignments will be made for implementation.

The following chart shows the nine different processes that make up the firm. The result of the 2006 fall retreat was a very complete understanding of what it would take to successfully implement key strategic initiatives. Decisions were then made as to which initiatives to pursue and what resources were needed for success. This provided detailed input to the operational planning process.

For 2007, the theme for the planning meetings was refinement of corporate goals and development of seven things that were necessary to achieve the goals. Also, the idea of the Rotex "story" was introduced to help communicate the goals and the means to achieve them to the employees. The summary notes from the early summer meeting follow the process flowchart to provide a more specific idea of the result of that meeting as well.

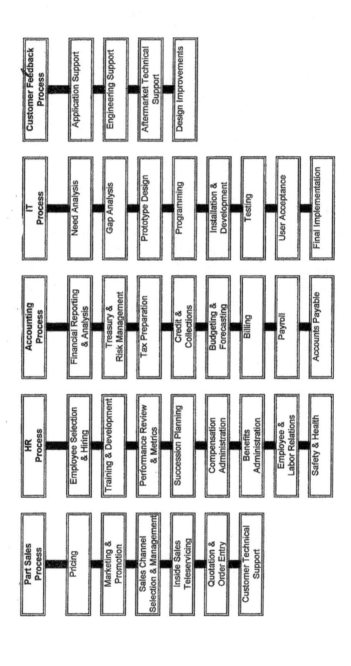

Part Sales Process
- Pricing
- Marketing & Promotion
- Sales Channel Selection & Management
- Inside Sales Teleservicing
- Quotation & Order Entry
- Customer Technical Support

HR Process
- Employee Selection & Hiring
- Training & Development
- Performance Review & Metrics
- Succession Planning
- Compensation Administration
- Benefits Administration
- Employee & Labor Relations
- Safety & Health

Accounting Process
- Financial Reporting & Analysis
- Treasury & Risk Management
- Tax Preparation
- Credit & Collections
- Budgeting & Forecasting
- Billing
- Payroll
- Accounts Payable

IT Process
- Need Analysis
- Gap Analysis
- Prototype Design
- Programming
- Installation & Development
- Testing
- User Acceptance
- Final Implementation

Customer Feedback Process
- Application Support
- Engineering Support
- Aftermarket Technical Support
- Design Improvements

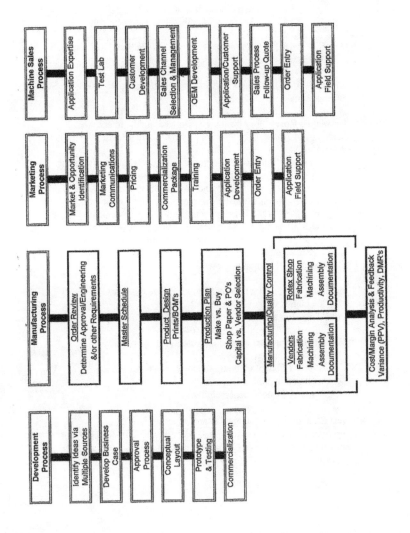

Machine Sales Process
- Application Expertise
- Test Lab
- Customer Development
- Sales Channel Selection & Management
- OEM Development
- Application/Customer Support
- Sales Process Follow-up Quote
- Order Entry
- Application Field Support

Marketing Process
- Market & Opportunity Identification
- Marketing Communications
- Pricing
- Commercialization Package
- Training
- Application Development
- Order Entry
- Application Field Support

Manufacturing Process
- Order Review Determine Approval/Engineering &/or other Requirements
- Master Schedule
- Product Design Prints/BOM's
- Production Plan Make vs. Buy Shop Paper & PO's Capital vs. Vendor Selection
- Manufacturing/Quality Control
  - Vendors Fabrication Machining Assembly Documentation
  - Rotex Shop Fabrication Machining Assembly Documentation
- Cost/Margin Analysis & Feedback Variance (PPV), Productivity, DMR's

Development Process
- Identify Ideas via Multiple Sources
- Develop Business Case
- Approval Process
- Conceptual Layout
- Prototype & Testing
- Commercialization

S8 Preparation Meeting Minutes
May 21, 2007

Attendees: Sid Barton, W. Herkamp, W. Lower, B. Ballman, K. Maurer, M. Moore, R. Paulsen, C. Sims, G. Armstrong

1. Reviewed Individual input on what our Strategic Goals should be. See scanned notes from 5/21.

2. Developed Rotex Story from discussion and inputs to achieve outcomes of Doubling Top line in 5 years, Share growth and EBITDA growth.
   a. Through Product Development and Acquisition, provide our customer's the optimal dry separation solution. Identify and document the processes and procedures that make us Number 1 in the USA and transfer these processes to Europe to achieve comparable Market share and Profitability as compared to the U.S. Implement Pricing strategies that reflect our Value Proposition. Expand into other international markets growing these markets, with year over year operational improvements leading to profitable growth.

3. Identified 7 things that needed to happen to achieve or Goals:
   a. Establish "Rotex" Culture in Europe
   b. Selection and Development of People
   c. Develop Marketing Strategy (4-P's)
   d. Identifying next Product Development opportunity
   e. Global Enterprise System
   f. DFM, Efficient Operating Plan, Product and Process Standardization.
   g. Project/Product responsibility

4. Next Step, during remaining day and a half we will take approximately 1 ½ hours to discuss these seven items with goal for prioritizing and identifying most critical issues and assignments for presentation and discussion in August.

5. See attached notes.

G Armstrong

For 2008, the theme was a better understanding of markets and competitors. Assignments were made to research the geographic and application markets for the firm to refine understanding and serve as a better basis for sales and marketing resource deployment. Further, assignments were made to research the key competitors identified to anticipate responses and take advantage of weaknesses. At the fall planning meeting, individuals were required to take the role of the competitive firm they had researched and make a "strategy" presentation. This exercise revealed significant information not previously recognized and allowed for actions to be developed to counteract potential competitive threats.

While details are not shown here, each year the basic strategic statement elements and related assumptions were reviewed and refined as well. However, the major work focused on the themes that were felt to be most important to the success of the enterprise. The result was an engaged strategy team that was challenged to produce meaningful information each year that would impact resource allocation decisions.

Bill Herkamp's assessment of the value of the process follows.

Commentary by Mr. Bill Herkamp, CEO

One of the more difficult aspects of strategic planning is to keep the process fresh and the ideas flowing. Too often the process becomes "institutionalized," which can result in the planning process becoming burdensome and the plan being uninspiring and poorly executed. Unfortunately, many outside facilitators are trained in teaching a process but do not instill in their clients the tools that encourage real strategic thinking. Having a formal process in place is important, but it must encourage and reward learning to assure the best outcome.

In one of our first meetings with Dr. Barton, he challenged each of the team members to explain the meaning of the Rotex vision and mission statements that had been communicated to our employees over the past ten years. The responses clearly highlighted how easy it is to assume understanding and agreement. This simple request resulted in our spending many hours debating the meaning of almost every single word until we got agreement. The consensus developed during that exercise now drives our product development, marketing, and acquisition efforts as well as almost every other functional area of the company.

One of the major improvements made to our strategic planning process through our association with Dr. Barton deals with our critical thinking. Every strategic action has its foundation built upon assumptions and market intelligence that are not 100 percent fact based. It is imperative to recognize which of these assumptions are truly critical to the success or failure of the action. Once you have made this determination you must vigorously test and retest their validity. You must, as Dr. Barton states in this book, "encourage and allow creative conflict," even with the CEO.

Developing a sound strategic management system is one of the key contributors to our explosive growth over the past five years. It has allowed the management of Rotex to efficiently focus its resources on the best growth opportunities. It has forced us to "benchmark" each opportunity against a template of specific criteria so that everyone in the organization needs to answer critical questions about opportunities, such as does it help us move toward achieving our mission and vision statements, does it build upon our core strengths, and is it compatible with our overall corporate strategy.

Bottom-line, our strategic management system has helped us to select the best growth opportunities available to the company and stay on task to achieve the return. As I have often been reminded, "Good results without good planning come from good luck rather than good management."

Epilogue

The examples shown and the comments from the CEOs responsible for implementing strategic management in their organizations are as varied as the organizations and their environments. What is common, however, is the fundamental managerial belief system that underlies their approaches. They initially bought into and eventually applied in their own ways the approaches outlined in this book. Further, they all agreed that the result of this application resulted in significant improvement in performance.

Mr. Bowers went considerably beyond the others in discussing how he not only applied the approaches to his example firm but how he successfully took these principles to subsequent firms. His point that implementation of the approach differed in each case as the context and culture of the organizations differed provides a powerful validation of the thesis of this book. The process may have been different for each organization, but the underlying philosophy remained unchanged, effective, and relevant.

As my mother said many years ago, "The proof is in the pudding." As it relates to strategic management, I believe the real-life case studies provide evidence for the effectiveness and universality of the principles and approaches outlined in this book.

As with the CEOs in the examples above, I sincerely hope that you also find the material helpful in your goal of making your organization the best it can be through truly effective strategic management.

Bibliography

Amason, Allen C. (1996). "Distinguishing the effects of functional and dysfunctional conflict on strategic decision making: Resolving a paradox for top management teams, *Academy of Management Journal* 39(1): 123–148.

Amatucci, Frances M., & Grant, John H. (1993). "Eight strategic decisions that weakened Gulf Oil," *Long Range Planning* 26(1): 98–110.

Andersen, Torben Juul (2000). "Strategic planning, autonomous actions and corporate performance," *Long Range Planning* 33(2): 184–200.

Andersen, Torben Juul (2004). "Integrating decentralized strategy making and strategic planning processes in dynamic environments," *Journal of Management Studies* 41(8): 1271–1299.

Andrews, Kenneth Richmond (1980). *The Concept of Corporate Strategy*. Homewood, IL: Richard D. Irwin.

Case, John (1996). *Open-Book Management: The Coming Business Revolution*. New York: Harper Collins Publishers.

Coyne, Kevin P., & Horn, John (2009). "Predicting your competitor's reaction," *Harvard Business Review* 87(4): 90–97.

Dialectical approaches. Mycoted Web site: http://www.mycoted.com/Dialectical_Approaches.

Dooley, Robert S., Fryxell, Gerald E., & Judge, William Q. (2000). "Belaboring the not-so-obvious: Consensus, commitment and strategy implementation speed and success," *Journal of Management* 26(6): 1237–1257.

Floyd, Steven W., & Wooldridge, Bill (1994). "Dinosaurs or dynamos? Recognizing middle management's strategic role," *Academy of Management Executive* 8(4): 47–57.

Floyd, Steven W., & Wooldridge, Bill (1997). "Middle management's strategic influence and organizational performance," *Journal of Management Studies* 34(3): 465–487.

Gerbing, David W., Hamilton, Janet G., & Freeman, Elizabeth B. (1994). "A large-scale second-order structural equation model of the influence of management participation on organizational planning benefits," *Journal of Management* 20(4): 859–885.

Kim, W. Chan, & Mauborgne, Renee A. (1998). "Procedural justice, strategic decision making and the knowledge economy," *Strategic Management Journal* 19(4): 323–338.

Knott, Paul (2008). "Strategy tools: Who really uses them?" *Journal of Business Strategy* 29(5): 26–31.

Mazzola, Pietro, Marchisio, Gaia, & Astrachan, Joe (2008). "Strategic planning in family business: A powerful development tool for the next generation," *Family Business Review* 21(3): 239–258.

Miller, Danny (1993). "The architecture of simplicity," *Academy of Management Review* 18(1): 116–138.

Mitroff, Ian I., & Emshoff, James R. (1979). "On strategic assumption-making: A dialectical approach to policy and planning," *Academy of Management Review* 4(1): 1–12.

Porter, Michael E. (1980). *Competitive Strategy: Techniques for Analyzing Industries and Competitors*. New York: Free Press.

Tregoe, B., & Zimmerman, J. (1980). *Top Management Strategy: What It Is and How to Make It Work*. New York: Simon and Schuster.

Zwahlen, Cyndia. (2000). "Company ledger an open book," *Los Angeles Times*, December 20, 2000. Quote from Karen Berman, founder of the Business Literacy Institute in West Los Angeles.

About the Author

Dr. Sidney L. Barton began his professional career as an engineer, working for an engineering consulting and software firm. He worked his way up to a position as the youngest vice president of the firm and worked a total of thirteen years at the company, which averaged 40 percent per year sales growth during that period. Sid founded and became general manager of the company's sales division, where he was responsible for the firm's sales and strategic planning. Supported by the firm's founder, he took his young family to Bloomington, Indiana, for three years in pursuit of a doctorate in strategic management, with a minor in finance. After completing the doctorate, Sid took a tenure-track position at the University of Cincinnati and successfully pursued an academic research and publication career. He has taught countless students and executives and consulted with dozens of organizations during the past twenty-four years. This experience as practitioner, researcher, teacher, and consultant has given Sid a unique and rich perspective on the process of strategic management, which has informed the contents of this book.

CPSIA information can be obtained
at www.ICGtesting.com
Printed in the USA
LVHW092151260520
656627LV00003B/13/J

9 781440 194221